HARVARD ORIENTAL SERIES

Edited by MICHAEL WITZEL

VOLUME EIGHTY-ONE

Materials Towards the Study of Vasubandhu's Viṁśikā (I)

Sanskrit and Tibetan Critical Editions of the Verses and Autocommentary, An English Translation and Annotations

by

JONATHAN A. SILK

PUBLISHED BY THE DEPARTMENT OF SOUTH ASIAN STUDIES

HARVARD UNIVERSITY

DISTRIBUTED BY HARVARD UNIVERSITY PRESS,

CAMBRIDGE, MASSACHUSETTS

AND LONDON, ENGLAND

2016

Printed in the United States of America

Published with the generous assistance of the *J. Gonda Fund* Foundation.
This book is printed in the Brill font, through the kind permission of
Koninklijke Brill NV

For information write to Editor, Harvard Oriental Series, Department of South Asian Studie
1 Bow Street, Cambridge MA 02138, USA
617-495 3295; email: witzel@fas.harvard.edu

Library of Congress Cataloguing in Publication Data
Materials Toward the Study Of Vasubandhu's *Viṁśikā* (I).
Sanskrit and Tibetan Critical Editions of the Verses and Autocommentary. An English Translation and Annotations

Harvard Oriental Series; v. 81. ISBN 978-0674970670

I. Jonathan A.Silk, 1960-
II. Title
III. Series: Harvard Oriental Series; 81
CIP

Materials Toward the Study of Vasubandhu's *Viṁśikā*

(I)

Sanskrit and Tibetan Critical Editions

of the

Verses and Autocommentary

An English Translation

and

Annotations

Table of Contents

Introduction

In 1912 Louis de La Vallée Poussin published an edition of the Tibetan translation of Vasubandhu's *Viṁśikā* and its autocommentary (on the title, see below), accompanied by an annotated French translation, deeply informed by his profound learning. In 1925, thanks to a discovery in Nepal, Sylvain Lévi was able to publish the Sanskrit of the same text (1925a), which he followed with a French translation (1932). Lévi, however, was constrained to work primarily with a hand-copy, and a number of textual problems remained. In the decades since, although all based on Lévi's edition, a number of editions and translations have been published, representing efforts to come to grips with what seems at first glance like a small and simple text. But as many scholars have discovered, while small, it is anything but simple. A great aid toward the further study of the text was made in 1989 by the publication by Mimaki, Tachikawa and Yuyama of (black and white) photographs of the unique palm leaf manuscripts, preserving both the verses and the author's autocommentary. When I first took up work on these manuscripts, I was not aware of any published studies. In the intervening years, however, at least two have appeared, Balcerowicz and Nowakowska (1999) and Tola and Dragonetti (2004). Unfortunately, neither of these efforts is fully satisfactory (neither, moreover, took any serious account of the Tibetan translations). Although I prepared an edition and translation years ago, I hesitated to publish it, due to my conviction that without a thorough study not only of the Chinese translations, but also, crucially, of the commentaries, the text in its traditional understanding would remain plagued with problems.

Having reached the conclusion, however, that I was unlikely to be able in the foreseeable future to assemble the team of specialists necessary to adequately engage, most importantly, with the commentaries, preserved only in Tibetan and Chinese, I decided to concentrate on Vasubandhu's texts, to produce critical editions of the Tibetan versions of the verses and autocommentary and to present them alongside my edition of the Sanskrit text. I have renounced for the present my idea to accompany these with editions of the Chinese translations, since the problems presented even by the translation of Xuanzang (see below) would have both swelled the work beyond a reasonable size, and delayed its presentation indefinitely. (The other two Chinese translations confront us with even greater challenges.) Of the accuracy of the Sanskrit and Tibetan editions presented below I am more or less confident—meaning that even if I have not understood and emended the texts correctly, at least I have reported their readings accurately. Of the accompanying English translation, I remain in some spots in doubt. It illustrates my understanding, to be sure, but that understanding is anything but firm in more than one place—despite the kind and generous help I have received from a number of friends and colleagues who have been willing, over the years, to offer suggestions on these materials.

It is a genuine pleasure, now precisely 90 years after the publication of Lévi's *editio princeps*, to offer a reedition of this fundamental text. I have read it with students, and presented it at a Leiden Linguistics Summer School, and I thank all who partcipated. One draft was read by Jowita Kramer, whom I thank for her good suggestions. Lambert Schmithausen, with his characteristic charity and humility, shared "some haphazardly noted stray remarks." These many comments—surely needless to say—vastly improved the presentation. In the very few instances when I have still, stubbornly, disagreed with Prof. Schmithausen, I have given my reasons in the notes. Finally, with his well-known generosity my old friend Harunaga Isaacson, joined by Mattia Salvini, carved out some time to go over the Sanskrit edition with me, and this had—again, needless to say—very positive results. It need hardly be emphasized that none of those who have so generously offered advice is in any way responsible for the errors that remain, but these friends and colleagues are severally and collectively certainly to be credited with any merits the present work may have. In conclusion, I thank Prof. Michael Witzel for doing me the honor of including this volume in the Harvard Oriental Series.

*

In the materials presented here, my editions of the *kārikās* alone, and of the integral text with its commentary, are based for the Sanksrit respectively on manuscripts A (3a4-4a5) and B (in its entirety) published by Mimaki, Tachikawa and Yuyama (1989). I am grateful for the advice on decipherment and other matters given by Diwakar Acharya during the above-mentioned course in which I taught the text in Leiden in 2007. For the Tibetan, I have utilized the following editions of the Tanjur:

For the *Viṁśikā-kārikā* (*nyi shu pa'i tshig le'ur byas pa*):

Cone: *sems tsam, shi* 3a4-4a2.
Derge 4056: *sems tsam, shi* 3a4-4a2.
Ganden 3556: *sems tsam, si* 4a3-5a5.
Narthang 4325: *sems tsam, si* 4a5-5a5.
Peking 5557: *sems tsam, si* 3b1-4b1.

For the *Viṁśikā-vṛtti* (*nyi shu pa'i 'grel pa*):

Cone: 3557, *sems tsam, si* 4a2-10a3.
Derge 4057: *sems-tsam, shi* 4a3-10a2.
Ganden 3557: *sems tsam, si* 5a5-13a5.
Narthang 4326: *sems tsam, si* 5a5-10b7.
Peking 5558: *sems tsam, si* 4b1-11a1.

As one would expect, Cone and Derge almost always agree against Ganden, Narthang and Peking. However, this does not mean that the readings of the former are always to be preferred, although they often are. In at least three places, it is clear that all editions have perpetuated an error (XV [B], XIX [G], XIV [I]).

Alongside the 'canonical' Tibetan translation of the verses, we are also lucky to have what plainly represents an earlier form of the translation, preserved in a single manuscript found at Dunhuang, now kept in Paris as Pelliot tibétain 125 (below, PT 125). This was recorded by Lalou (1939: 43) as follows:

1) *Viṁśikākākikā* (*biṅ çi ka / ka ri ka*). *Ñi-çu-pa dgos-par byed-pa'o.* Complet? fin: *ñi-çu-pa rjogso.* Cf. *Tanǰur*, Mdo LVII,2.
2) *Triṁśikākārikā* (*triṅ çi ka / ka ri ka*). *Sum-čhu-pa dgos-pa byed-pa'o.* Cf. *Tanǰur*, Mdo, VVII, 1.

3 f. (7.4 x 28.2) non pag.; 6.1, règl. estampées, petites marges noires, trou à gauche non cerclé; ponct. inters. avec deux points. Papier pelucheux.

I will have nothing further to say here about the *Triṁśikā*, but the entire manuscript was earlier transcribed by Ueyama (1987). On the basis of color photographs available on the Artstor website, I have reread the former portion of the manuscript, containing the verses of the *Viṁśikā*, and been able to correct a few of Ueyama's readings. I agree with the following important conclusions offered by Ueyama: copyist errors prove that this manuscript is not an original or fair-copy coming from the translator's pen, but a copy of another manuscript. The similarity of the text to that eventually established in the Tanjurs shows that this version does not represent a different text or translation altogether, but is an earlier form of the later revised translation. There is no chance that it was translated from Chinese. (Ueyama is more cautious, saying that it is not made at least from any of the presently known Chinese versions, but as I show below, errors in understanding of the Sanskrit prove that its direct source must have been in Sanskrit.)

Although I have remarked on some points of interest in the notes to the edition, here I wish to point out some of the peculiarities of this version, in light of both the Sanskrit text and the 'canonical' translation. The first is that unlike the *Vṛtti*, but like the independent translation of the verses in the Tanjurs and Manuscript A of the Sanskrit, PT 125 contains the first verse. This verse also reveals the oddity that PT 125, which elsewhere translates *vijñapti* with *rnam shes*, here renders it *rnam rig*. When *vijñāna* appears in verse 6, PT 125 renders this too with *rnam par shes pa*, the (later?) standard translation equivalent. Further evidence for the copying of PT 125 is found in 1d, which is unmetrical. We might presume that *skra zla la stsogs pa myed mthong bas so* should be understood *skra zla lastsogs pa myed mthong baso*, which would provide (graphically at least) seven syllables. Finally, I do not understand *shes bya ba*, normally *iti*, in 1a; was what is now *evedam* in Sanskrit somehow written in a way that led the Tibetan translators to understand an *iti* there? Verse 2 illustrates the fact that PT 125 follows the Sanskrit word order slavishly; this is particularly clear in d where *vijñaptir yadi nārthataḥ* appears as *rnam shes +on te don myed na+o*. (I do not understand what it means that this verse is followed not by a double shad, as is normal, but by something resembling |༶|). A number of other examples of literal rendition of Sanskrit word order are to be found throughout

Verse 15, besides proving that it is based on a Sanskrit (rather than Chinese) original, provides an extreme illustration of the fact that the text in PT 125 required revision. The first line alone contains nothing but errors: the Sanskrit text has *ekatve na krameṇetir*, 'If [the sense object] were singular, there would be no gradual motion,' which PT 125 renders *gchigis dang nï rims zhes pa*. Here *gchigis* [*gcig gis*] = **ekatvena* in place of *ekatve na*, and *rims zhes pa* = **kramena iti*, understanding *iti* as the quotative particle rather than as a verb (the second member of the compound is perhaps more commonly spelt *eti* than *iti*; for the grammar see Verhagen [1996: 28; 40n96], and my note to this passage). This word evidently motivated some possible misunderstanding in India as well, since the manuscript of the *Vṛtti* includes what I understand as a gloss in XV (C), *gamanam ity arthaḥ*, which would not be necessary unless the word *iti/eti* was liable to misunderstanding. While a detailed study of PT 125 must await another occasion, it is certain that the text recorded in PT 125 (although to be sure not this precise manuscript version) stood behind the revision later enshrined in the Tanjurs. Moreover, that this older version was in some way available at least to the translators of the *Vṛtti* in its unrevised form is shown by 20d, in which the *Vṛtti* preserves the reading of PT 125 against that in the Tanjur version of the kārikās.

The present work is nothing more than one step toward a more satisfactory and wholistic philological treatment of the *Viṁśikā* (to say nothing of a contextualized philosophical study). What has not been taken into account in this treatment of the text are its Chinese translations (with only a few exceptions in the notes), and its commentaries, which comprise the following sources:

Weishi lun 唯識論, T. 1588, translated by Prajñāruci 瞿曇般若流支.
Dasheng weishi lun 大乘唯識論,T. 1589, translated by Paramārtha.
Weishi ershi lun 唯識二十論, T. 1590, translated by Xuanzang. (On these three, with the Tibetan translation, see inter alia Sasaki 1924 and Akashi 1926)
Dharmapāla's *Cheng weishi baosheng lun* 成唯識寶生論, T. 1591, translated by Yijing 義淨 (see Liebenthal 1935).
[Kui] Ji's [窺]基 *Weishi ershilun shuji* 唯識二十論述記, T. 1834 (see in part Hamilton 1938).
Vinītadeva's *Prakaraṇaviṁśakaṭīkā, Rab tu byed pa nyi shu pa'i 'grel bshad,* Derge 4065, *sems tsam, shi* 171b7-195b5 (see Yamaguchi and Nozawa 1953: 1-131, and Hillis 1993).
Vairocanarakṣita's subcommentary on Vinītadeva, *Viṁśikāṭīkā-vivṛti,* edited in Kano 2008.

Concerning the proper title of the work, it has long been referred to in modern scholarship as the *Viṁśatikā*, a mistake found in the Sanskrit manuscript of the *Vṛtti* which has at last been corrected by Kano (2008: 350. Note however that Lévi (1925b: 17) does already call the text "Viṁśatikā ou Viṁśikā"). Aside from the detailed Pāṇinian analysis provided by Vairocanarakṣita, as Kano points out there has long been abundant evidence for the correct title *Viṁśikā*. This includes a Chinese transcription in [Kui]Ji's commentary, and Tibetan transcriptions. In this regard, we should note that *pace* Kano, the Tanjurs do not read *viṅśika* (or even *biṅśika*) but rather clearly they have only a single vowel in almost all cases, therefore yielding at best *viṅśaka*, perhaps not coincidentally the reading of the colophon in MS (A), *viṁśakā-vijñaptiprakaraṇaṁ*, and that contained at least in the Derge edition's title of Vinītadeva's commentary, *Prakaraṇaviṅśakaṭīkā*. It is interesting to note that in PT 125, although Lalou read *bing*, a comparison with other examples of vowels on the same folio shows that it is only possible to understand here *beng*. We should also note that the Tanjurs have the Tibetan title of the verses as *nyi shu pa'i tshig le'ur byas pa*, while PT

125 has instead *nyï shu pa dgos par byed pa+o*. Here *dgos par byed pa* seems to be an attempt to etymologically render *kārikā*, connecting it with the root √*kṛ*. I have not found this elsewhere.

I have imposed the sentence numbering on the text in an effort to make comparison between versions, and reference to the translation, more transparent. The identification of objections in the translation owes much to the commentaries, but I hasten to emphasize that I have not made a proper study of these, and this aspect of the work (as so much else) must remain highly provisional. I have retained in so far as practical the punctuation of the Sanskrit manuscript, although it must be admitted that the result often seems somewhat inconsistent.

The *Viṁśikā* has been translated into modern languages a number of times. Among the best efforts may be that of Frauwallner (1994: 366-383; 2010: 392-411), and I have profited much from consulting it. A step toward further improved understanding of thc text will involve close study of both the Chinese translations, and the commentaries, listed above.

The text has been often studied by modern scholars, but I make no pretence here to contribute to the doctrinal, philosophical or historical study of the text (see recently the very interesting Kellner and Taber 2014). I am, moreover, aware that Vasubandhu's text probably had significant influence on later works (such as Dharmakīrti's *Santānāntarasiddhi*; see Yamabe 1998). My notes attempt to do no more than provide clues focused, in the first place, on philologically relevant aspects of the establishment of the Sanskrit text, rather than engagement with the text's contents *per se*. It would thus be otiose here to attempt a (perforce very partial) listing of relevant studies on the doctrine of the *Viṁśikā*.

I adopt the following conventions:

Tibetan:

I do not distinguish between *pa/ba*, or *nga/da*, selecting in all cases the 'correct' form.

I ignore for the most part Narthang's frequent abbreviated spellings, such as *seṁn* for *sems can*, *rnaṁr* for *rnam par* and so on.

I mostly do not note minor orthographic oddities which may be due to breaks on the printing blocks (missing vowels, for instance).

In PT 125, I may have been ungenerous to the scribe; he writes *pa/pha* almost identically, and unless I am sure he intended *pha*, I transcribe this letter as *pa*.

ï transcribes the reversed *gi-gu* (*gi gu log*).

+ transcribes the *'a-rten* with a flag on its right shoulder འ.

Sanskrit:

(*Italics*) within parenthesis in the Sanskrit text indicate a reconstruction based on Tibetan and context. These usually but not always agree with the suggestions of Lévi.

[ ] Brackets in the Sanskrit indicate a partially legible character.

⟨ ⟩ Angle brackets indicate a supplement to the text.

+ A + indicates a missing letter, the number determined by the available space in the manuscript.

. One dot indicates either a consonant or a vowel missing.

* An asterisk after a letter indicates that the manuscript has a special form of the letter which does not include a vowel, or a virāma (typically with t and sometimes ṁ).

Bold characters indicate the first akṣara on a line of the manuscript.

Folio numbers are supplied in small notation to indicate folio and side.

When I have altered the text more than to make a trivial correction, I make a note on the same page. All changes, even trivial, are noted in the apparatus.

Punctuation marks are as in the manuscript, unless otherwise noted. The *daṇḍa* is indicated with | , half *daṇḍa* (rare) with ╷, a mark more or less like ╷、 with ; , and one more or less like 、 with , .

When *avagraha* is not written in the manuscript, as needed I add it between ⟨ ⟩; in other cases, I transcribe it as written in the manuscript.

Literature

Akashi Etatsu 明石恵達. 1926. *Zōkan Wayaku Taikō Nijū Yuishikiron Kaisetsu* 藏漢和譯對校 二十唯識論解說 (Kyoto: Ryūkoku Daigaku Shuppanbu 龍谷大學出版部. Reprint: Tokyo: Daiichi shobō 第一書房, 1985).

Balcerowicz, Piotr, and Monika Nowakowska. 1999. "Wasubandhu: „Dowód na wyłączne istnienie treści świadomości w dwudziestu strofach" (*Viṁśatikā – Vijñapti-mātratā-siddhi*)." *Studia Indologiczne* 6: 5-44.

Bendall, Cecil. 1897–1902. *Çikshāsamuccaya: A Compendium of Buddhistic Teaching Compiled by Çāntideva, Chiefly from Earlier Mahāyāna-sūtras.* Bibliotheca Buddhica 1 (St. Pétersbourg: Imperial Academy. Reprint: Osnabrück: Biblio Verlag, 1970).

Chu, Junjie. 2004. "A Study of *Sataimira* in Dignāga's Definition of Pseudo-Perception (PS 1.7cd–8ab)". *Wiener Zeitschrift für die Kunde Südasiens* 48: 113–149.

Chu, Junjie. 2011. "Sanskrit Fragments of Dharmakīrti's *Santānāntarasiddhi.*" *Religion and Logic in Buddhist Philosophical Analysis: Proceedings of the Fourth International Dharmakirti Conference Vienna, August 23–27, 2005* (Vienna: Verlag der Österreichischen Akademie der Wissenschaften): 33–42.

Chung, Jin-il, and Takamichi Fukita. 2011. *A Survey of the Sanskrit Fragments Corresponding to the Chinese Madhyamāgama: Including References to Sanskrit Parallels, Citations, Numerical Categories of Doctrinal Concepts, and Stock Phrases* (Tokyo: Sankibo Press).

Dutt, Nalinaksha. 1939. *Gilgit Manuscripts* 1. Kashmir Series of Texts and Studies 71,1. (Srinagar and Calcutta: J. C. Sarkhel at the Calcutta Oriental Press).

Edgerton, Franklin. 1953. *Buddhist Hybrid Sanskrit Dictionary* (New Haven: Yale University Press).

Frauwallner, Erich. 1994. *Die Philosophie des Buddhismus.* 4th ed. (Berlin: Akademie Verlag).

Frauwallner, Erich. 2010. *The Philosophy of Buddhism.* Trans. Gelong Lodrö Sangpo with the assistance of Jigme Sheldrön, under the supervision of Professor Ernst Steinkellner (Delhi: Motilal Banarsidass).

Funahashi Naoya 舟橋尚哉. 1986. "Nepāru shahon taishō ni yoru *Yuishiki Sanjūju* no gentenkō narabi ni *Yuishiki Nijūron* daiichige dainige no genpon ni tsuite" ネパール写本対照による『唯識三十頌』の原典考並びに『唯識二十論』第一偈第二偈の原本について [Textual notes on the Triṃśikāvijñaptibhāṣyaṃ based on the Comparison of Nepalese

Manuscripts and a Study of Verses 1 and 2 of the Viṃśatikā]. *Bukkyōgaku Seminā* 仏教学セミナー 43: 15–30.

Gnoli, Raniero. 1978. *The Gilgit Manuscript of the Sanghabhedavastu, part 2*. Serie Orientale Roma 49 / 2 (Rome: IsMEO).

Hahn, Michael. 2011. "The Tibetan Shes rab sdong bu and its Indian Sources (III)." *Minami Ajia Kotengaku* 南アジア古典学 (= *South Asian Classical Studies*) 6: 305–378.

Hamilton, Clarence Herbert. 1938. *Wei Shih Er Lun, or, The Treatise in Twenty Stanzas on Representation-Only*. American Oriental Series 13 (New Haven: American Oriental Society).

Hanneder, Jürgen. 2007. "Vasubandhus *Viṃśatikā* 1–2 anhand der Sanskrit- und tibetischen Fassungen." In Konrad Klaus and Jens-Uwe Hartmann, eds., *Indica et Tibetica. Festschrift für Michael Hahn, zum 65. Geburtstag von Freunden und Schülern überreicht*. Studien zur Tibetologie und Buddhismuskunde 66 (Vienna: Studien zur Tibetologie und Buddhismuskunde): 207–214.

Harada Wasō 原田和宗. 1999. "*Yuishiki Nijūron* nōto 1: sono tekusuto kōtei to kaishakugakujō no shomondai" 『唯識二十論』ノート (1): そのテクスト校訂と解釈学上の諸問題 [A Philological and Doctrinal Reconsideration of the *Viṁśatikā Vijñaptimātratāsiddhi*, Part 1]. *Bukkyō Bunka* 仏教文化 (Kyūshū Ryūkoku Tanki Daigaku Bukkyō Bunka Kenkyūjo 九州龍谷短期大学 仏教文化研究所) 9: 101–131.

Harada Wasō 原田和宗. 2000. "*Yuishiki Nijūron* nōto 2" 『唯識二十論』ノート (2) [A Philological and Doctrinal Reconsideration of the *Viṁśatikā Vijñaptimātratāsiddhi*, Part 2]. *Kyūshū Ryūkoku Tanki Daigaku Kiyō* 九州龍谷短期大学紀要 46: 173–190.

Harada Wasō 原田和宗. 2003. "*Yuishiki Nijūron* nōto 3" 『唯識二十論』ノート (3) [A Philological and Doctrinal Reconsideration of the *Viṁśatikā Vijñaptimātratāsiddhi*, Part 3]. *Kyūshū Ryūkoku Tanki Daigaku Kiyō* 九州龍谷短期大学紀要 49: 131–188.

Hillis, Gregory. 1993. An Introduction and Translation of Vinitadeva's Explanation of the First Ten Verses of (Vasubandhu's) Commentary on his 'Twenty Stanzas' with Appended Glossary of Technical Terms. MA thesis, University of Virginia.

Hinüber, Oskar von. 2014. "The Gilgit Manuscripts: An Ancient Buddhist Library in Modern Research. In Paul Harrison and Jens-Uwe Hartmann, eds., *From Birch Bark to Digital Data: Recent Advances in Buddhist Manuscript Research*. Beiträge zur Kultur- und Geistesgeschichte Asiens 80; Denkschriften der philosophisch-historische Klasse 460 (Vienna: Verlag der Österreichischen Akademie der Wissenschaften): 79–135.

Honjō Yoshifumi 本庄良文. 2014. *Kusharonchū Upāyikā no Kenkyū* 倶舎論註ウパーイカーの研究 (Tokyo: Daizō shuppan 大蔵出版).

Ichigo, Masamichi. 1989. "Śāntarakṣita's *Madhyamakālaṁkāra*: Introduction, Edition and Translation." In Luis O. Gómez and Jonathan A. Silk, eds., *Studies in the Literature of the Great Vehicle: Three Mahāyāna Texts* (Ann Arbor: Collegiate Institute for the Study of Buddhist Literature and Center for South and Southeast Asian Studies, The University of Michigan): 141-240.

Jha, Ganganatha. 1919. *The Nyāyasūtras of Gautama with Vātsyāyana's Bhāṣya and Uddyotkara's Vārṭika*. Vol. IV: Comprising Adhyāya IV and V. 'Indian Thought' Series 13 (Allahabad: Belvedere Steam Printing Works).

Kano, Kazuo. 2008. "Two Short Glosses on Yogācāra texts by Vairocanarakṣita: *Viṁśikāṭīkāvivṛti* and **Dharmadharmatāvibhāgavivṛti*." In Francesco Sferra, ed., *Sanskrit Texts from Giuseppe Tucci's Collection*. Part I. Manuscripta Buddhica 1. Serie Orientale Roma 104 (Rome: Istituto Italiano per l'Africa e l'Oriente): 343–380.

Kellner, Birgit, and John Taber. 2014. "Studies in Yogācāra-Vijñānavāda Idealism I: The Interpretation of Vasubandhu's *Viṁśikā*." *Asiatische Studien / Études Asiatiques* 68/3: 709–756.

La Vallée Poussin, Louis de. 1901–1914. *Bodhicaryāvatārapañjikā, Prajñākaramati's Commentary to the Bodhicaryāvatāra of Çāntideva*. Bibliotheca Indica 983, 1031, 1090, 1126, 1139, 1305, 1399 (Calcutta: Asiatic Society).

La Vallée Poussin, Louis de. 1901–1902. "Le Bouddhisme d'après les sources brahmaniques." *Le Muséon* N.S. 2: 52–73, 171–207; N.S. 3: 40–54, 391–412.

La Vallée Poussin, Louis de. 1903–1913. *Mūlamadhyamakakārikās* (*Mādhyamikasūtras*) *de Nāgārjuna avec la Prasannapadā Commentaire de Candrakīrti*. Bibliotheca Buddhica 4 (St. Pétersbourg: Imperial Academy. Reprint: Osnabrück: Biblio Verlag, 1970).

La Vallée Poussin, Louis de. 1912. "Vasubandhu Viṁśakakārikāprakaraṇa. Traité des Vingt ślokas, avec le commentaire de l'auteur." *Le Muséon* 13: 53–90.

La Vallée Poussin, Louis de. 1923–1931. *L'Abhidharmakośa de Vasubandhu* (Paris: Geuthner. Reprint: *Mélanges chinois et bouddhiques* 16, Bruselles: Institut Belge des hautes Études Chinoises, 1971).

Lalou, Marcelle. 1939. *Inventaire des Manuscrits tibétains de Touen-houang conservés à la Bibliothèque Nationale*, (Fonds Pelliot tibétain) no. 1–849. (Paris: Maisonneuve; Bibliothèque Nationale).

Lee, Jong Cheol. 2005. *Abhidharmakośabhāṣya of Vasubandhu: Chapter IX: Ātmavādapratiṣedha*. Bibliotheca Indologica et Buddhologica 11 (Tokyo: The Sankibo Press).

Lévi, Sylvain. 1908. "Açvaghoṣa, le Sūtrālaṃkāra et ses sources." *Journal Asiatique* 12 (2nd ser.): 57–184.

Lévi, Sylvain. 1925a. *Vijñaptimātratāsiddhi: Deux Traités de Vasubandhu: Viṁśatikā (La Vingtaine), Accompagnée d'une explication en prose, et Triṁśikā (La Trentaine), avec le Commentaire de Sthiramati. Original Sanscrit Publié pour la premiére fois d'après des manuscrites rapportés du Népal.* Bibliothèque de l'École des Hautes Études, Sciences historiques et philologiques 245 (Paris: Librairie Ancienne Honoré Champion).

Lévi, Sylvain. 1925b. "Notes Indiennes. I: Deux notes sur la Viṁśatikā de Vasubandhu: 1. La défaite de Vemacitra; 2. Un fragment de l'Upāli sūtra en Sanscrit." *Journal Asiatique* 206: 17–35.

Lévi, Sylvain. 1932. *Matériaux pour l'Étude du Système Vijnaptimātra.* Bibliothèque de l'École des Hautes Études, Sciences historiques et philologiques 260 (Paris: Librairie Ancienne Honoré Champion).

Liebenthal, Walter. 1935. "The Version of the Viṁśatikā by I-ching and its Relation to that of Hsüan-tsang." *Yenching Journal of Chinese Studies* (*Yanjing Xuebao* 燕京學報) 17: 179–194.

Mimaki, Katsumi, Musashi Tachikawa, and Akira Yuyama, eds. 1989. *Three Works of Vasubandhu in Sanskrit Manuscript: The* Trisvabhāvanirdeśa, *the* Viṁśatikā *with its* Vṛtti, *and the* Triṁśikā *with Sthiramati's Commentary.* Bibliotheca Codicum Asiaticorum 1. (Tokyo: The Centre for East Asian Cultural Studies).

Nasu Jisshū 那須実秋. 1953. "Yuishiki Nijūron no kanbon" 唯識二十論の還梵 [The Sanskrit reconstruction of the Viṁśikā]. *Indogaku Bukkyōgaku Kenkyū* 印度学仏教学研究 3/2: 113–114.

Pradhan, Prahlad. 1975. *Abhidharmakośabhāṣyam of Vasubandhu.* Tibetan Sanskrit Works 8 (Patna: K. P. Jayaswal Research Institute).

Sasaki Gesshō 佐々木月樵. 1924. *Yuishiki Nijūron no Taiyaku Kenkyū* 唯識二十論の對譯研究 (Kyoto: Naigai Shuppan 内外出版. Reprinted with notes by Yamaguchi Susumu 山口益: Tokyo: Kokusho Kankōkai 国書刊行会, 1977).

Silk, Jonathan A. 2016. "A Tibetan Grammatical Construction: verb + *na go*." *Revue d'Etudes Tibétaines* 35 (Forthcoming April 2016).

Suali, Luigi. 1905. "Il 'Lokatattvanirṇaya' di Haribhadra." *Giornale della Società Asiatica Italiana* 18: 263–319.

Tarkatirtha, Amarendramohan, and Hemantakumar Tarkatirtha, eds. 1944. *Nyāya-darśanam: with Vātsyāna's Bhāṣya, Uddyotakara's Vārttika, Vācaspati Miśra's Tātparyaṭīkā & Viśvanātha's Vṛtti.* Calcutta Sanskrit Series 29 (Calcutta: Metropolitan Printing & Publishing House).

Tola, Fernando, and Carmen Dragonetti. 2004. *Being as Consciousness: Yogācāra Philosophy of Buddhism* (Delhi: Motilal Banarsidass).

Ueyama Daishun 上山大峻. 1987. "Tonkō shutsudo Chibetto iyaku *Yuishiki Nijūju Yuishiki Sanjūju*: P.tib.125" 敦煌出土・チベット異訳『唯識二十頌』『唯識三十頌』: P.tib.125 [Tibetan Manuscript from Tun-huang; newly identified as the Viṃśatikā and the Triṃśikā]. In Ryūkoku Daigaku Bukkyō Gakkai 龍谷大学仏教学会, ed., *Yuishiki Shisō no Kenkyū: Yamazaki Keiki Kyōju Teinen Kinen Ronshū* 唯識思想の研究 山崎慶輝教授定年記念論集 (Kyoto: Hyakkaen 百華苑) (= *Bukkyōgaku Kenkyū* 仏教学研究 43): 546–528 (1–19).

Ui Hakuju 宇井伯壽. 1917. "'Yuishiki' no gengo ni tsuite." 『唯識』の原語について [On the word Weishi]. *Tetsugaku Zasshi* 哲學雜誌, reprinted in *Indo Tetsugaku Kenkyū* 印度哲学研究 1 (Kōshisha shobō 甲子社書房, 1925): 1–7.

Ui Hakuju 宇井伯壽. 1953. *Shiyaku Taishō Yuishiki Nijūron Kenkyū* 四譯對照唯識二十論研究 (Tokyo: Iwanami shoten 岩波書店).

Verhagen, Peter Cornilius. 1996. "Tibetan Expertise in Sanskrit Grammar – a Case Study: Grammatical Analysis of the Term Pratitya-Samutpada." *Journal of the Tibet Society* 8: 21–48.

Wogihara Unrai 荻原雲來. 1936. *Sphuṭārthā Abhidharmakośavyākhyā: The Work of Yaśomitra* (Reprint: Tokyo: Sankibo Buddhist Book Store, 1989).

Yamabe, Nobuyoshi. 1998. "Self and Other in the Yogācāra Tradition." *Nihon Bukkyō Bunkaronsō: Kitabatake Tensei Hakushi Koki Kinen Ronbunshū* 日本佛教文化論叢: 北畠典生博士古稀記念論文集 (Kyoto: Nagata Bunshōdō 永田文昌堂): 15–41.

Yamaguchi Susumu 山口益 and Nozawa Jōshō 野澤靜證. 1953. *Seshin Yuishiki no Genten Kaimei* 世親唯識の原典解明 (Kyoto: Hōzōkan 法藏館).

Chinese texts are cited according to the Taishō edition.

Pāli texts are referred to in the Pali Text Society editions, with the standard sigla.

Tibetan sigla:

C: Cone Tanjur
D: Derge Tanjur
G: Golden (Ganden) Tanjur
N: Narthang Tanjur
P: Peking Tanjur

Sanskrit Manuscript A

Tibetan Tanjur Critical Edition

and

Pelliot tibétain 125

of the

Viṁśikā-kārikā

With an English Translation

Viṁśikā-Kārikā

	Sanskrit Text	Tanjur	PT 125
	In principle, manuscript A	C: Cone D: Derge G: Ganden (Golden) N: Narthang P: Peking	
0	namaḥ sarvvajñāya ||	rgya gar skad du | bingsha ka kā ri ka | bod skad du | nyi shu pa'i tshig le'ur byas pa | | 'jam dpal gzhon nur gyur pa la phyag 'tshal lo ||	༄།ཿ། rgya gar kyï skad du beng shï ka | ka rï ka || || bod skad du nyï shu pa dgos par byed pa+o ||
		a: bingsha] Written བིངྴ in all versions kā ri ka] C: kā ri kā b: byas pa ||] CDN: byas pa |	

1	vijñaptimātram evedam asadarthāva- bhāsanāt* | yadvat taimirakasyāsatkeśoṇḍūkādi- darśanam* ||	'di dag rnam par rig tsam nyid || yod pa ma yin don snang phyir || dper na rab rib can dag gis || skra zla la sogs med mthong bzhin ||	༄ : || rnam rig tsam ste shes bya ba || myed pa+ï don snang ba+ï phyiro || ji ltar rab rib can gyisu || skra zla la stsogs pa myed mthong bas so ||
			c: can] MS cin with i vowel cancelled
	Not in the *Vṛtti.*		shes bya ba = ?

This [world] is just Manifestation-Only,
because of the appearance of non-existent external objects,
as in the case of the seeing of nonexistent hair-nets and the like
by one with an eye disease.

2	na deśakālaniyamaḥ santānāniyamo na [ca] | na ca kṛtyakriyā yuktā vijñaptir yadi nārthataḥ ||	gal te rnam rig don min na || yul dang dus la nges med cing || sems kyang nges med ma yin la || bya ba byed pa'ang mi rigs 'gyur ||	yul dang dus la chad pa myed || rgyud kyang ma chad ma yïn zhing || bya ba byed pa yang rïgs pa myed || rnam shes +on te don myed na+o |∷|
			b: rgyud] MS rgud
			rgyud = santāna (sems) chad = niyama (nges) rnam shes = vijñapti (but in 1a rnam rig; below = vijñāna) +on te = yadi, following Sanskrit word order don myed na = nārtha (don min na)

If manifestation does not [arise] from an external object,
it is not reasonable that there be restriction as to time and place,
nor nonrestriction as to personal continuum,
nor causal efficacy.

3	deśādiniyamaḥ siddhaḥ svapnavat pretavat punaḥ | santānāniyamaḥ sarvvaiḥ pūyanadyādi-darśane ||	yul la sogs pa nges 'grub ste || rmi 'dra'o sems kyang nges pa med || yi dags bzhin te thams cad kyis || klung la rnag la sogs mthong bzhin ||	yul la stsogs pa chad grub ste rmï +dra+o || yï dags bzhïn du yang || ma chad rgyud do thams chad dag || rnag chu la stsogs mthong baso ||
		c: yi dags] G yi dwags	c: ma chad rgyud] MS ma chad ~~do~~ rgyud
			rnag chu = pūyanadī (klung la rnag)

Restriction as to place and so on is proved,
as with dreams.
Moreover, nonrestriction to personal continuum [is proved] as with hungry ghosts,
in their all seeing the river of pus and so on.

<table>
<tr><td>4</td><td>svapnopaghātavat kṛtyakriyā narakavat punaḥ |
sarvvan narakapālādidarśane taiś ca bādhane ||</td><td>bya byed rmi lam gnod pa ’dra ||
thams cad sems can dmyal ba bzhin ||
dmyal ba’i srung ma sogs mthong dang ||
de dag gis ni gnod phyir ro ||</td><td>rmi lam gnod pa +dra bya ba dang ||
bya+o sems dmyal bzhin du yang ||
kun de sems dmyal srung la stsogs ||
mthong zhing de+is bda+ baso ||</td></tr>
<tr><td></td><td></td><td>d:
de dag gis] G: de dag gi</td><td>b:
Ueyama read bye’i = byed’i, but it is clearly bya+o
d:
zhing de+is] MS zhing ~~pa~~ de+is</td></tr>
<tr><td></td><td></td><td></td><td>bda’ ba [to chase] ≠ bādhane (gnod). (In a, both have gnod = upaghāta)</td></tr>
<tr><td colspan="4">Causal efficacy [is proved] as in ejaculation in a dream.
And again as with hell all [four aspects are proved],
in the seeing of the hell guardians and so on,
and in being tortured by them.</td></tr>
</table>

5	tiraścāṁ sambhavaḥ svargge yathā na narake tathā | na pretānāṁ yatas tajjan duḥkhan nānu-bhavanti te ||	ji ltar dud ’gro mtho ris su || ’byung ba de ltar dmyal ba min || yi dags min te ’di lta bur || de yod sdug bsngal des mi myong ||	byol songs mtho ris +byung ba dag || jï bzhin sems dmyal myed de bzhïn || myï +dre gang las der skyes gyi || sdug bsngal myï myong de de dago ||
	b: yathā na] MS (A) erroneously yathā ca d: duḥkhan] MS (A) written duṣkhan or duḥkhan	c: yi dags] G yi dwags min te] C: min ta	b: dmyal] MS dmyu̶l
		Vṛtti in c: de for ’di	byol songs = tiraśca (dud ’gro) +dre = preta (yi dags) gang las = yataḥ de dag = te

Animals are not born in hell
as they are in heaven,
nor are hungry ghosts,
since they do not experience the suffering produced there.

6	yadi tatkarmmabhis tatra bhūtānāṁ sam- bhavas tathā | iṣyate pariṇāmaś ca kiṁ vijñānasya neṣyate ||	gal te de yi las kyis der || ’byung ba dag ni ’byung ba dang || de bzhin ’gyur bar ’dod na go || rnam par shes par cis mi ’dod ||	de ste de+ï las gyis der || +byung ba dag de bzhïn du || +dod ching +gyur ba rnams kyang na || rnam par shes pa jir myi +dod ||
		a: de yi] GN: de’i	de+ï] MS da+ï der] MS red
		Vṛtti in a: de’i for de yi	

If you accept that gross material elements arise there
in this fashion through the karmic deeds of those [beings],
and [you accept their] transformation,
why do you not accept [the transformation] of cognition?

7	karmmaṇo vāsanānyatra phalam anyatra kalpyate | tatraiva neṣyate yatra vāsanā kin nu kāraṇaṁ ||	gzhan na las kyi bag chags la || 'bras bu dag ni gzhan du rtog | gang na bag chags yod pa der || ci yi phyir na 'dod mi bya ||	las kyï bag chags gzhan du la || +bras bu dag nï gzhan du rtog || gang na ba der myi +dod na || bag chags ji+i phyir zhig du ||
		Vṛtti in d: ci'i for ci yi	

The perfuming of the karmic deed
you imagine to be elsewhere than the result;
What is the reason you do not accept [that
the result is] in precisely the same location where the perfuming [takes place]?

8	rūpādyāyatanāstitvan tadvineyajanam prati | abhiprāyavaśād uktam upapādukasatvavat* ||	gzugs sogs skye mched yod par ni || des 'dul ba yi skye bo la | dgongs pa'i dbang gis gsungs pa ste || rdzus te 'byung ba'i sems can bzhin ||	gzugs stsogs +du mched yod par nï || des gdul +gro ba dag la +o | dgongs pa+ï dbang gis | gsungs pa ste || rdzu ba+ï sems chan bzhin ||
		b: 'dul ba yi] G: 'dul ba ni	
			+du mched ≠ āyatana (skye mched; homonym 'du byed normally = saṁskāra) +gro ba = jana (yi skye); dag suggests plural?
The existence of the sense-fields of material form and the rest were spoken of [by the Blessed One] with a special intention directed toward the individual to be guided by that [teaching], as [in the case of the mention of] beings born by spontaneous generation.			

9	yataḥ svabījād vijñaptir yadābhāsā pravarttate | dvividhāyatanatvena te tasyā munir abravīt* ||	rang gi sa bon gang las su || rnam rig snang ba gang 'byung ba || de dag de yi skye mched ni || rnam pa gnyis su thub pas gsungs ||	gang bdag sa bon las rnaṁ shes || gang snang rab du +jug pa nï || +du mched rnam pa gnyis pasna || de dag de+ir thub pas gsungs ||
	d tasyā] MS (A) ac tasyā plus an extra (unnecessary, hence erased) vertical line for long vowel		
		Vṛtti in b: 'byung for byung	rab du +jug pa = pravartate ('byung ba)

A manifestation arises from its own proper seed,
having an appearance corresponding to that [external object].
The Sage spoke of the two [seed and appearance]
as the dual sense field of that [manifestation].

10	tathā pudgalanairātmyapraveśo hy anyathā punaḥ | deśanā dharmmanairātmyapraveśaḥ kalpitātmanā ||	de ltar gang zag bdag med par || 'jug par 'gyur ro gzhan du yang || bstan pas chos la bdag med par || 'jug 'gyur brtags pa'i bdag nyid kyis ||	de ltar gang zag bdag myed par || +jug pa+o gang pyïr gzhan phyïr yang || bshad pa chos la bdag med par || +jug pa brtags pa bdagïs so
	cd dharmanairātmya°] MS (A) dharmmyanairātmya°	b: 'jug par] C: jug par	
		Vṛtti in c: bstan pa'i (D: bstan pa)	bshad pa = deśanā (bstan pa)

For in this way there is understanding of the selflessness of persons.
Moreover, teaching in another way
leads to the understanding of the selflessness
of the elemental factors of existence in terms of an imagined self.

11	na tad ekaṁ na cānekaṁ viṣayaḥ paramāṇuśaḥ | na ca te saṁhatā yasmāt paramāṇur na sidhyati ||	de ni gcig na'ang yul min la || phra rab rdul du du ma'ang min || de dag 'dus pa 'ang ma yin te || 'di ltar rdul phran mi 'grub phyir ||	de ni myï gchig du ma+ang myed || yul nï rdul pran dagïso || de bsdus myïn gang phyï ru || rdul pran myï +grub pa+ïs so ||
	d paramāṇur na] MS (A) erroneously adds ca in margin by na	c: pa'ang ma] N: pa'i ngam	

That [sense-field of form and the rest] is not a unitary
nor atomically plural sense object,
neither are those [atoms] compounded,
since the atom [itself] is not proved.

12	ṣaṭkena yugapadyogāt paramāṇoḥ ṣaḍaṁśatā | ṣaṇṇāṁ samānadeśatvāt piṇḍaḥ syād aṇu- mātrakaḥ ||	drug gis cig car sbyar ba na || phra rab rdul cha drug tu 'gyur || drug po dag ni go gcig na || gong bu rdul phran tsam du 'gyur ||	drugïs chig char ldan bas na || rdul phran cha nï drug du+o || drug rnams mnyam ba+ï yul bas na || gong bu rdul tsam du +gyur ba+o ||
	a yugapadyogāt] MS (A) yugpadayogāt		
		Vṛtti in a: sbyar bas na In c: drug po dag kyang go gcig na	ldan ba = yoga (sbyar ba) mnyam ba+ï yul ba = amānadeśa (go gcig)

Because [either] in the simultaneous conjunction with a group of six [other atoms],
the atom [would have to] have six parts.
[Or] because, the six being in a common location,
the cluster would be the extent of a [single] atom.

13	paramāṇor asaṁyoge tatsaṁghāte ⟨'⟩sti kasya saḥ | na cānavayavatvena tatsaṁyogo na sidhyati ||	rdul phran sbyor ba med na ni || de 'dus yod pa de gang gis || cha shas yod pa ma yin pas || de sbyor mi 'grub ma zer cig ||	rdul pran myï +du ba yïn na || de+i bsdus yod su+ï de+ || bag bag kyang ma yïn | myïn bas || de+i +du ba myï +grubo |
	c na] MS (A) ac nā d tatsaṁyogo na sidhyati] MS (A) ac repeats tatsaṁyogo na sidhyati.		
		ma zer cig = ? ('do not say!'). In prose (B) = *na vaktavyam.*	+du ba = saṁyoga (sbyor ba) bag bag = anavaya ? (cha shas)

Given that there is no conjunction of atoms,
what is [conjoining] when those [atoms] are compounded?
But it is also not due to their partlessness
that the conjunction of those [atoms] is not proved.

14	digbhāgabhedo yasyāsti tasyaikatvaṁ na yujyate | chāyāvr̥tī kathaṁ vānyo na piṇḍaś cen na tasya te ||	gang la phyogs cha tha dad yod || de ni gcig tu mi rung ngo || grib dang sgrib par ji ltar 'gyur || gong bu gzhan min de de'i min ||	pyogs cha tha dad gang yod pa || de+i gchig du myï rung ngo || drib dang sgrib kyang ji ltar | +gyur || pung myin gal te de de myin ||
	c chāyāvr̥tī] MS (A) °vr̥ttī c vānyo na] MS vā anyonya; MS (A) syātāṁ na d cen na] MS (A) nna added below the line > MS (A): In the margin below tāṁ na pi in another (more modern) hand is written mi li tā. Harunaga Isaacson suggests that this (as militāḥ) may be a gloss on piṇḍa: '[the atoms] connected/combined'.	b: de ni] N: da ni	
			pung (phung) = piṇḍa (gong bu)

It is not reasonable that something with spatial differentiation be singular.
Or how is there shadow and obstruction?
If the cluster is not other [than the atoms],
the two [shadow and obstruction] would not be [properties] of that [cluster].

15	ekatve na krameṇetir yugapan na grahāgrahau | vicchinnānekavr̥ttiś ca sūkṣmānīkṣā ca no bhavet* ||	gcig na rim gyis 'gro ba med || zin dang ma zin cig car med || ris chad du mar gnas pa dang || mig gis mi gsod phra ba'ang med ||	gchigis dang nï rims zhes pa || gchïg char bzung dang ma bzung myed || bar chad du ma +jug pa dang || phra dang myi mthong myed par +gyurd ||
	a krameṇetir] MS (A) krameṇeti d sūkṣmā°] Both MSS śūkṣmā°	a: gcig na] CD: gcig ni b: zin cig] CD: zan cig d: mi gsod] CD: mi sod	
		mar gnas pa = ? *Vr̥tti* in d: *mi sod* (N *mi bsod*). mig gis mi gsod: in the *Vinayasūtra-vyākhyāna* of Prajñākara (Derge Tanjur 4121, *'dul ba, ru* 122b1) we find: *mthong ba'o zhes pa yin te mig gis gsod pa'i srog chags yod na gdod nyes par 'gyur ba'o.*	gchigis = ekatvena! (≠ ekatve na) rims zhes pa = krameṇa iti! (≠ krameṇetiḥ) bzung dang ma bzung = grahāgraha (zin dang ma zin) bar chad du = vicchinna (ris chad du) ma +jug pa = ? myi mthong = anīkṣa (≠ mig gis mi gsod; what is gsod?)

If [the sense object] were singular,
there would be no gradual motion,
no simultaneous apprehension and non-apprehension,
nor divided multiple existence, nor the invisible microscopic.

16	pratyakṣabuddhiḥ svapnādau yathā sā ca yadā tadā | na so ⟨'⟩rtho dṛśyate tasya pratyakṣatvaṁ katham mataṁ ||	mngon sum blo ni rmi sogs bzhin || de yang gang tshe de yi tshe || khyod kyi don de mi snang na || de ni mngon sum ji ltar 'dod ||	rmï laṁ stsogs mngon sum blo || jï ltar de+ang gang tshe de+i tshe || de+i de dag don myi snang || mngon sum du nï ji ltar phye ||
	a pratyakṣabuddhiḥ] MS (A) °buddhi b tadā] MS (A) ac tādā	c: khyod kyi don] D: khyod kyi den	a: blo] MS lo c: de+i tshe] MS de+i tshe ~~de~~
			phye = mata?

The idea that there is direct perception [of the external object takes place] as in a dream and so on.
Additionally, that external object is not seen [at the moment]
when one has [the idea that there is direct perception of an external object];
[so] how can you consider that [the external object] is directly perceived?

17	uktaṁ yathā tadābhāsā vijñaptiḥ smaraṇan tataḥ | svapnadṛgviṣayābhāvan nāprabuddho vagacchati ||	dper na der snang rnam rig bzhin || bshad zin de las dran par zad || rmi lam mthong ba yul med par || ma sad bar du rtogs ma yin ||	smras pa gang tshe de+is snang na nï || rnam par shes pas dran baso || rmyï laṁ mthong bas yul myed par || ma sad par nï myi chud do ||
	b vijñaptiḥ] MS (A) vijñapti d nāprabuddho] MS (A) nāpraṁbuddho	d: ma sad] G: ma zad	
			gang tshe ≠ yathā (rather = *yadā) chud = avagacchati (rtogs)
As I discussed, manifestation has the appearance of that [external object]. Recollection [comes] from that. One who is not awake does not understand the non-existence of a sense-object seen in a dream.			

18	anyonyādhipatitvena vijñaptiniyamo mithaḥ | middhenopahataṁ cittaṁ svapne tenāsamaṁ phalaṁ ||	gcig la gcig gi dbang gis na || rnam par rig pa phan tshun nges || sems ni gnyid kyis non pas na || de phyir rmi dang 'bras mi mtshungs ||	gchig la gchigi dbang gïs na || rnam shes chad pa pan tshun tu+o || gnyid gyïs nye bar non pa+ï sems || rmi lam de dang +bras myi mnyam ||
	b mithaḥ] MS (A) mitha, with tha overwritten.	a: gis na] C: gi ni	b: chad pa] MS interlinear addition below c: bar] ba+ï written, +ï cancelled and ra added below ba
Mutual shaping of manifestation is due to their influence on each other. When one dreams, the mind is overpowered by sloth; thus the result is not the same.			

19	maraṇaṁ paravijñaptiviśeṣād vikriyā yathā | smṛtilopādikānyeṣāṁ piśācādimanovaśāt ||	'chi ba gzhan gyi rnam rig gis || bye brag las te dper bya na || 'dre la sogs pa'i yid dbang gis || gzhan gyi dran nyams 'gyur sogs bzhin ||	gsod pa gzhan gyi rnam shes gyi || bye bragis pye ji lta bar || gzhan gyï dran ba nyams par gyurd || sha za la stsogs pa+ï dbang gis ||
	a maraṇaṁ] MS (A) maraṇa	a: rig gis] P: rigs gis b: dper bya na] N: dpang byin? d: nyams] N: nyis?	
		yid dbang = manovaśa (PT 125 omits an equivalent for manas)	gsod pa = maraṇa ('chi ba) sha za= piśāca ('dre)

Death is a transformation due to a particular manifestation
of another, just as the transformation
of memory loss and the like of others
is due to the mental force of demons and so on.

20	kathaṃ vā daṇḍakāraṇyaśūnyatvam ṛṣikopataḥ | manodaṇḍo mahāvadyaḥ kathaṁ vā tena sidhyati ||	drang srong khros pas dan ta ka'i || dgon pa ji ltar stongs par 'gyur || yid nyes kha na ma tho cher || de yis ji ltar 'grub par 'gyur ||	dbyig pa+i dgon pa ji ltar na || drang srong khros pas stong pa bar || yïd gyis nyes pa sdig tshe bar || ji ltar de+is grub pa yïn ||
		a: khros] N: bros dan ta] GNP: dante b: stongs par 'gyur] GNP: stong par gyur d: de yis] CD: de mis	d: grub] MS ~~bs~~grub
		Vṛtti in d: ji ltar de yis 'grub par 'gyur NB: this reading ≈ PT 125!	dbyig pa = daṇḍa nyes pa sdig tshe ba = mahāvadyaḥ (kha na ma tho cher)

Otherwise, how did the Daṇḍaka forest become emptied by the sages' anger?
Or how does that prove mental violence is a great violation?

<table>
<tr><td>21</td><td>paracittavidāṁ jñānam ayathārthaṁ kathaṁ yathā |
svacittajñānam ajñānād yathā buddhasya gocaraḥ ||</td><td>gzhan sems rig pa'i shes pa ni ||
don bzhin ma yin ji ltar dper ||
rang sems shes pas sangs rgyas kyi ||
spyod yul ji bzhin ma shes phyir ||</td><td>pha rol sems rïg pa+is shes ||
jï bzhin myï don jï +ji ltar ||
bdagï sems shes myï shes pas ||
ji ltar sangs rgyas spyod yulo ||</td></tr>
<tr><td></td><td>b
ayathārthaṁ] MS (A) rtha overwritten, no ṁ visible
c
ajñānād] MS (A) adds °nā° in top margin with ˇ</td><td>a:
rig pa'i] CD: rig pas
b:
ma yin] N: ma</td><td></td></tr>
<tr><td></td><td></td><td>Vṛtti in a: sems rig pas (CD) or sems rigs pas (GNP)
in c: rang sems shes pa</td><td>pha rol sems = paracitta (gzhan sems)
jï bzhin myï don = ayathārtha (don bzhin ma yin)
bdagï sems = svacitta (rang sems)</td></tr>
<tr><td colspan="4">How is the knowledge of those who know other minds inconsistent with reality?
[Reply:] It is as with knowledge of one's own mind.
Because one does not know [other minds or even one's own]
in the way that [such knowing of minds] is the scope of a Buddha.</td></tr>
</table>

22	vijñaptimātratāsiddhiḥ svaśaktisadr̥śī mayā | kr̥teyaṁ sarvvathā sā tu na cintyā buddha- gocaraḥ ||	rnam rig tsam du grub pa 'di || bdag gis bdag gi mthu 'dra bar || byas kyi de yi rnam pa kun || bsam yas sangs rgyas spyod yul lo ||	rnam shes tsam du +grub paru || bdagïs bdagï mthu +dra bas +dï bgyis rnam pa thams chad de+o || sangs rgyas spyod yul bsam du med || ||
	c kr̥teyaṁ] MS (A) kr̥tyeyaṁ		
			rnam pa thams chad = sarvathā (rnam pa kun) bsam du med = na cintya (bsam yas)

I have composed this proof of [the World as] Manifestation-Only according to my ability,
but that [fact that the World is nothing but Manifestation-Only]
is not conceivable in its entirety.
It is the scope of the buddhas.

C	viṁśakāvijñaptiprakaraṇaṁ samāptam* || śloka 20	nyi shu pa'i tshig le'ur byas pa slob dpon dbyig gnyen gyis mdzad pa rdzogs so || || rgya gar gyi mkhan po dzi na mi tra dang | shī len dra bo dhi dang dā na shī la dang | zhu chen gyi lo tsā ba ban de ye shes sdes bsgyur cing zhus te gtan la phab pa'o ||	nyi shu pa rdzogso ||
	20] MS (A) written as 2 with ṁ above The following namaḥ sarvvavide || no doubt belongs with the following Triṁśikā-kārikā.	shī] N: shi len dra] GN: lendra; P: landra bo dhi dang] CD: bo dhi dang | tsā] N: tsa ban de] GNP: bande	
		The Twenty Verses written by the Venerable Vasubandhu. Translated by the Indian masters Jinamitra, Śīlendrabodhi and Dānaśīla, and the great translator Ye shes sde, it has been corrected.	

Sanskrit Manuscript B

and

Tibetan Tanjur Critical Edition

of the

Viṁśikā-vṛtti

With an English Translation

0

rgya gar skad du | bingshi ka brītti ||
bod skad du | nyi shu pa'i 'grel pa |
'jam dpal gzhon nur gyur pa la phyag 'tshal lo ||

I

A) theg pa chen po la khams gsum pa rnam par rig pa tsam du rnam par gzhag ste | B) mdo las | kye rgyal ba'i sras dag 'di lta ste | khams gsum pa 'di ni sems tsam mo zhes 'byung ba'i phyir ro || C) sems dang yid dang | rnam par shes pa dang | rnam par rig pa zhes bya ba ni rnam grangs su gtogs pa'o || D) sems de yang 'dir mtshungs par ldan pa dang bcas par dgongs pa'o || E) tsam zhes bya ba smos pa ni don dgag pa'i phyir ro || F) rnam par shes pa 'di nyid don du snang ba 'byung ste | G) dper na rab rib can rnams kyis skra zla la sogs pa med par mthong ba bzhin te | H) don gang yang med do ||

I

.... H) nārthaḥ kaścid asti |

[Vasubandhu]

A) The Great Vehicle teaches that what belongs to the triple world is established as Manifestation-Only, because it is stated in scripture: B) "O Sons of the Conqueror, what belongs to the triple world is mind-only." C) Mind, thought, cognition and manifestation are synonyms. D) And here this 'mind' intends the inclusion of the concomitants [of mind]. E) "Only" is stated in order to rule out external objects. F) This cognition itself arises having the appearance of an external object. G) For example, it is like those with an eye disease seeing non-existent hair, a [double] moon and so on, but H) there is no [real] object at all.

II

A) 'dir 'di skad ces brgal te |

gal te rnam rig don min na ||
yul dang dus la nges med cing ||
sems kyang nges med ma yin la ||
bya ba byed pa'ang mi rigs 'gyur || [2]

B) ji skad du bstan par 'gyur zhe na | C) gal te gzugs la sogs pa'i don med par gzugs la sogs pa'i rnam par rig pa 'byung ste gzugs la sogs pa'i don las ma yin na | D) ci'i phyir yul la lar 'byung la thams cad na ma yin | E) yul de nyid na yang res 'ga' 'byung la thams cad du ma yin | F) yul dang dus de na 'khod pa thams cad kyi sems la nges pa med pa 'byung la 'ga' tsam la ma yin | G) ji ltar rab rib can nyid kyi sems la skra la sogs pa snang gi | gzhan dag la ni ma yin ||

II

......

na deśakālaniyamaḥ santānāniyamo na [ca] |
na ca kr̥tyakriyā yuktā vijñaptir yadi nārthataḥ || 2 ||

[Objection:]

A) To this it is objected:

If manifestation does not [arise] from an external object, it is not reasonable that there be restriction as to time and place, nor nonrestriction as to personal continuum, nor causal efficacy. [2]

B) What is being stated here? C) If there is the arisal of manifestation of material form and so on without any external object of material form and so on, and [consequently the manifestation] does not [arise] from a [real] external object of material form and so on, D) why does [such a manifestation] arise in a particular place, and not everywhere; E) why does it arise only in that place at some time, not always; and F) why does it arise without restriction in the minds of all those present there in that place at that time, and not in [the minds] of just a few? G) For instance, while a hair and so on may appear in the mind of one with eye disease, it does not [appear] to others [free of that disease].

II

H) ci'i phyir gang rab rib can gyis mthong ba'i skra dang | sbrang bu la sogs pas skra la sogs pa'i bya ba mi byed la | de ma yin pa gzhan dag gis ni byed | I) rmi lam na mthong ba'i bza' ba dang btung ba dang bgo ba dang dug dang mtshon la sogs pas zas dang skom la sogs pa'i bya ba mi byed la | de ma yin pa gzhan dag gis ni byed | J) dri za'i grong khyer yod pa ma yin pas grong khyer gyi bya ba mi byed la | de ma yin pa gzhan dag gis ni byed | K) 'di dag don med par med du 'dra na yul dang dus nges pa dang | sems nges pa med pa dang | bya ba byed pa 'di dag kyang mi rung ngo zhe na |

II

K) ……-niyamaḥ santānāniyamaḥ kr̥tyakriyā ca na yujyate ,

H) Why is it that the hair, bee and so on which appear to one with eye disease have no causal efficacy of a hair and so on, while for those others without [eye disease, those hairs, bees and so forth which appear to them] do have [causal efficacy]? I) The food, drink, clothing, poison, weapons and so on seen in a dream do not have causal efficacy [to address] hunger, thirst and the like, but those others not [in a dream] do have such [causal efficacy]. J) A mirage city, being non-existent, does not have the causal efficacy of a city, but other [cities] not [unreal like] that do. K) If these [things like dream food] resemble the non-existent in lacking any [real external] object, restriction as to time and place,[1] nonrestriction as to personal continuum, and causal efficacy are not reasonable.

1: Here begins the Sanskrit manuscript; the translation hereafter is from the Sanskrit.

III

A) mi rung ba ma yin te | 'di ltar |

yul la sogs pa nges 'grub ste ||
rmi 'dra'o || [3ab]

B) rmi lam du rmis pa dang mtshungs pas na rmi 'dra'o || C) ji lta zhe na | D) rmi lam na yang don med par yul la la na grong dang | kun dga' ra ba dang | skyes pa dang bud med la sogs pa ji dag snang la thams cad na ma yin yul de nyid na yang res 'ga' snang la dus thams cad du ma yin pas E) don med par yang yul la sogs pa nges par 'grub po ||

D)
thams cad na ma yin yul de nyid na yang res 'ga' snang la] GNP: ø

III

A) na khalu na yujyate , yasmāt* ||

deśādiniyamaḥ siddhas svapnavat*

B) svapna iva svapnavat* ⟨ | ⟩ C) kathaṁ D) tāvat svapne vināpy arthena kvacid eva deśe **kiñcid** grāmārāmastrīpuruṣādikaṁ dr̥śyate na sarvatra tatraiva ca deśe kadācid dr̥śyate na sarvakālam E) iti siddho vināpy arthena deśakālaniyamaḥ ||

[Vasubandhu]

A) They are certainly not unreasonable, since:

Restriction as to place and so on is proved, as with dreams.

[3ab]

B) "As with dreams" means as in a dream. CD) Well, how, first of all, [do you explain that] even without an external object, some village, grove, man, woman or the like is seen in a dream at a particular place, rather than everywhere, and at that particular place at some specific time, rather than always? E) For this reason, restriction as to time and place is established, even in the absence of an external object.

D)
grāmārāmastrīpuruṣādikaṁ] MS: bhramarā°

III

sems kyang nges pa med |
yi dags bzhin te | [3bc]

F) grub ces bya bar bsnyegs so || G) yi dags rnams kyi dang mtshungs pas na yi dags bzhin no || H) ji ltar 'grub |

thams cad kyis |
klung la rnag la sogs mthong bzhin || [3cd]

III

pretavat punaḥ

santānāniyam**aḥ** ||

F) siddha iti vartate ; G) pretānām iva pretavat* | H) kathaṁ siddhaḥ | I) samaṁ

sarvaiḥ pūyanadyādidarśane || [3 ||]

Moreover, nonrestriction to personal continuum [is proved] as with hungry ghosts. [3bc]

F) "Is proved" is carried over [from the previous foot]. G) "As with hungry ghosts" means as in the case of hungry ghosts. H) How is this proved? I) Collectively

In their all seeing the river of pus and so on. [3cd]

III

J) rnag gis gang ba'i klung ni rnag gi klung ste | K) mar gyi bum pa bzhin no || L) las kyi rnam par smin pa mtshungs pa la gnas pa'i yi dags rnams ni kun gyis kyang mtshungs par klung rnag gis gang bar mthong ste | gcig 'gas ni ma yin no || M) rnag gis gang ba ji lta ba bzhin du gcin dang | ngan skyugs dang | me ma mur dang | mchil ma dang | snabs kyis gang ba dang | dbyig pa dang | ral gri thogs pa'i mi dag gis srung ba yang de bzhin te | sogs pa zhes bya bar bsdu'o || N) de ltar na don med par yang rnam par rig pa rnams kyi sems nges pa med par 'grub bo ||

III

J) pūyapūrṇṇā nadī pūyanadī | K) ghṛtaghaṭavat* | L) tulyakarmmavi**pā**kāvasthā hi pretāḥ sarve (')pi samaṁ pūyapūrṇṇān nadīm paśyanti naika eva | M) yathā pūyapūrṇṇām evaṁ mūtrapurīṣādipūrṇṇāṁ daṇḍāsidharaiś ca puruṣair adhiṣṭhitām ity ādi**gra**haṇena | N) evaṁ santānāniyamo vijñaptīnām asaty apy arthe siddhaḥ ||

J) "The river of pus" means a river filled with pus, K) as [one says] a pot of ghee [when one means a pot filled with ghee]. L) For hungry ghosts in a state of equally experiencing fruition of their actions collectively *all* see the river filled with pus, not just one of them alone. M) The word "and so on" is mentioned to indicate that as [they see the river] filled with pus, they [also see it] filled with urine, feces and the like, and guarded by persons holding staffs and swords. N) Thus the nonrestriction of manifestations to [a specific] personal continuum is proved even without the existence of an external object.

IV

bya byed rmi lam gnod pa 'dra || [4a]

A) grub ces bya bar rig par bya'o || B) dper na rmi lam na gnyis kyis gnyis phrad pa med par yang khu ba 'byung ba'i mtshan nyid ni rmi lam gyi gnod pa'o || C) de ltar re zhig dpe gzhan dang gzhan dag gis yul dang dus nges pa la sogs pa bzhi 'grub bo ||

IV

svapnopaghātavat kr̥tyakriyā |

A) siddheti veditavyaṁ* | B) yathā svapne dvayasamāpattim antareṇa śu**kra**visarggalakṣaṇaḥ svapnopaghātaḥ | C) evan tāvad anyānyair dr̥ṣṭāntair deśakālaniyamādicatuṣṭayaṁ siddhaṁ* |

Causal efficacy [is proved] as in ejaculation in a dream. [4ab]

A) "Is proved" is to be understood. B) [Causal efficacy is established] as with ejaculation in a dream [that is, a wet dream], which is characterized by the emission of semen in a dream in the absence of [actual] sexual union. C) In this way at the outset is proved, through these various examples, the four-fold [characterization, namely] the restriction to time and place and the rest.

C)
anyānyair] MS: anyānair

IV

thams cad sems can dmyal ba bzhin || [4b]

D) grub ces bya bar rig par bya'o || E) sems can dmyal ba dag na yod pa dang mtshungs pas sems can dmyal ba bzhin no || F) ji ltar 'grub ce na |

IV

narakavat punaḥ

sarvaṁ*

D) siddham iti veditavyaṁ | E) narakeṣv iva narakavat* 〈 | 〉 F) **ka**thaṁ siddhaṁ |

And again as with hell all [four aspects are proved]. [4bc]

D) "Are proved" is to be understood. E) "As with hell" means like in the hells. F) How are they proved?

IV

dmyal ba'i srung ma sogs mthong dang ||
de dag gis ni gnod phyir ro || [4cd]

G) dper na sems can dmyal ba dag na sems can dmyal ba'i sems can rnams kyis sems can dmyal ba'i srung ma la sogs pa mthong ste | yul dang dus nges par 'grub bo || H) khyi dang bya rog dang lcags kyi ri la sogs pa 'ong ba dang 'gro bar yang mthong ba ni sogs pa zhes bya bar bsdu ste | I) thams cad kyis mthong gi | gcig 'gas ni ma yin no || J) de dag gis de dag la gnod pa yang 'grub ste | dngos po la sems can dmyal ba'i srung ma la sogs pa med par yang rang gi las kyi rnam par smin pa mtshungs pa'i dbang gi phyir ro || K) de bzhin du gzhan yang yul dang dus nges pa la sogs pa bzhi po 'di dag thams cad grub par rig par bya'o ||

narakapālādidarśane taiś ca bādhane |[| 4 ||]

G) yathā hi narakeṣu nārakāṇāṁ narakapālādidarśanaṁ deśakālaniyamena siddhaṁ ⟨ | ⟩ H) śvavāyasāyasaparvatādyāgamanagamanada<2b1>rśanañ cety ādigrahaṇena ⟨ | ⟩ I) sarveṣāñ ca naikasyaiva ⟨ | ⟩ J) taiś ca tadbādhanaṁ siddham asatsv api narakapālādiṣu samānasvakarmmavipākādhipatyāt* | K) tathānyatrāpi sarvam etad deśakālaniyamādicatuṣṭayaṁ siddham iti veditavyaṁ* |

In the seeing of the hell guardians and so on, and in being tortured by them. [4cd]

G) Just as it is proved that in the hells hell beings see the hell guardians and so on with restriction as to time and place H) —"and so on" means that they see the dogs, crows, the iron mountains and so on coming and going— I) and all [hell beings see these], not merely one, J) and [just as it is] proved that they are tortured by them, even though the hell guardians and so on do not exist, because of the domination of the generalized common fruition of their individual karmic deeds— K) Just so it should be understood that the entirety of this four-fold [characterization, namely] the restriction to time and place and the rest, is proved elsewhere too [and not only in the separate examples].

IV

L) ci'i phyir sems can dmyal ba'i srung ma dang bya rog dang khyi la sogs pa de dag sems can du mi 'dod ce na |

M) mi rigs pa'i phyir ro || N) de dag ni sems can dmyal bar mi rigs te | de bzhin du sdug bsngal des mi myong ba'i phyir ro || O) gcig la gcig gnod pa byed na ni 'di dag ni sems can dmyal ba pa dag go || 'di dag ni sems can dmyal ba'i srung ma dag go zhes rnam par gzhag pa med par 'gyur ro || P) byad gzugs dang bong tshod dang stobs mtshungs pa dag ni gcig la gcig gnod pa byed kyang ji lta bur 'jigs par mi 'gyur ro || Q) lcags rab tu 'bar ba'i sa gzhi la tsha ba'i sdug bsngal yang mi bzod na ni ji ltar de na gzhan la gnod pa byed par 'gyur | R) sems can dmyal ba pa ma yin pa dag sems can dmyal bar 'byung bar ga la 'gyur |

IV

L) kim punaḥ kāraṇaṁ narakapālās te ca śvāno vāyasāś ca satvā neṣyante |

M) ayogāt* | N) na hi te nārakā yujyante tathaiva tadduḥkhāpratisamvedanāt* | O) parasparaṁ yātayatām ime nārakā ime narakapālā iti vyavasthā na syāt* | P) tulyākṛtipramāṇabalānāñ ca parasparaṁ yātayatān na tathā bhayaṁ syāt* | Q) dāhaduḥkhañ ca pradīptāyām ayomayyāṁ bhūmāv asahamānāḥ kathaṁ tatra parān yātayeyuḥ | R) anārakāṇāṁ vā narake kutaḥ sambhavaḥ ⟨ | ⟩

[Objection]

L) For what reason, then, do you not accept the hell guardians, and dogs and crows, as really existent beings?

[Vasubandhu]

M) Because it is not reasonable. N) For it is not reasonable for those [guardians and so on] to be hell beings, since they do not experience the sufferings of that [place] in precisely that same way. O) If they were torturing each other, there would be no differentiation that 'these are the hell beings; these the hell guardians.' P) And if those of equal form, size and strength were torturing each other, they would not be so very afraid. Q) And how could [those guardians], unable to tolerate the suffering of burning on a flaming iron ground, torture others there? R) On the other hand, how could non-hell beings be born in hell [in the first place]?

V

A) ’o na dud ’gro dag kyang ji ltar mtho ris su ’byung ste | B) de bzhin du sems can dmyal bar yang dud ’gro dang yi dags kyi bye brag sems can dmyal ba’i srung ma la sogs pa ’byung bar ’gyur ro zhe na |

V

A) kathan tāvat tiraścāṁ svarge sambhavaḥ | B) evaṁ **na**rakeṣu tiryakpretaviśeṣāṇāṁ narakapālādīnāṁ sambhavaḥ syāt* ||

[Objection]

A) [Well,] to begin, how [—as you admit as well—] could animals be born in heaven? B) In the same way, animals and certain hungry ghosts might be born in the hells as hell guardians and others.

V

ji ltar dud 'gro mtho ris su ||
'byung ba de ltar dmyal ba min ||
yi dags min te de lta bur ||
de yod sdug bsngal des mi myong || [5]

C) dud 'gro gang dag mtho ris su 'byung ba de dag ni snod kyi 'jig rten na de'i bde ba myong bar 'gyur ba'i las kyis der 'byung ba dag ste | de na yod pa'i bde ba so sor myong ngo || D) sems can dmyal ba'i srung ma la sogs pa dag ni de bzhin du sems can dmyal ba'i sdug bsngal mi myong ngo || E) de'i phyir dud 'gro dag der 'byung bar mi rigs so || F) yi dags kyi bye brag dag kyang ma yin no ||

V

tiraścāṁ sambhavaḥ svarge yathā na narake tathā |
na pretānāṁ yatas tajjaṁ duḥkhan nānubhava**nti** te || [5 ||]

C) ye hi tiryañcaḥ svarge sambhavanti te tadbhājanalokasukhasaṁvarttanīyena karmmaṇā tatra sambhūtās tajjaṁ sukhaṁ pratyanubhavanti | D) na caivan narakapālādayo nārakaṁ duḥ**khaṁ** pratyanubhavanti E) tasmān na tiraścāṁ sambhavo yukto F) nāpi pretānāṁ* ⟨ | ⟩

[Vasubandhu]

Animals are not born in hell as they are in heaven,
Nor are hungry ghosts, since they do not experience the suffering produced there. [5]

C) For, those who are born in heaven as animals, being born there through their karmic deeds conducive to happiness [performed] in the Receptacle World, experience the happiness produced there [in heaven], D) but the hell guardians and so on do not experience hellish suffering in a similar fashion. E) Therefore, it is not reasonable that animals are born [in hell], F) nor is it so for hungry ghosts.

VI

A) sems can dmyal ba de dag gi las rnams kyis der 'byung ba'i bye brag dag 'di lta bur 'byung ste | mdog dang byad gzugs dang bong tshod dang stobs kyi bye brag gang gis sems can dmyal ba'i srung ma la sogs pa'i ming thob pa'o || B) gang lag pa brkyang pa la sogs pa bya ba sna tshogs byed par snang ba de lta bur yang 'gyur ste | de dag 'jigs pa bskyed pa'i phyir ro || dper na lug lta bu'i ri dags 'ong ba dang | 'gro ba dang | lcags kyi shal ma li'i nags tshal tsher ma kha thur du lta ba dang gyen du lta bar 'gyur ba lta bu ste | C) de dag ni med pa yang ma yin no zhe na |

B)
'gyur] CD: 'grub

VI

A) teṣān tarhi nārakāṇāṁ karmmabhis tatra bhūtaviśeṣāḥ sambhavanti varṇṇākṛtipramāṇabalaviśiṣṭā ye naraka<3a1>**pālādi**saṁjñāṁ pratilabhante | B) tathā ca pariṇamanti yad vividhāṁ hastavikṣepādikriyāṁ kurvanto dṛśyante bhayotpādanārthaṁ yathā meṣākṛtayaḥ parvatā āgacchanto gacchantaḥ (*ayaḥśālmalī*)**vane** ca kaṇṭakā adhomukhībhavanta ūrddhamukhībhavantaś ceti | C) na te na sambhavanty eva ||

[Objection]

A) Then, particular types of gross material elements arise there through the karmic deeds of those hell beings, which, particularized as to color, form, size and strength, obtain the designations 'hell guardian' and so on. B) And they transform in such a manner that they appear performing activities like waving their hands and so on, in order to instill fear, as mountains in the shape of rams coming and going and thorns in the forest of iron thorn trees turning themselves down and turning themselves up [likewise appear in hell instilling fear]. C) Therefore, it is not that those [hell guardians and so on] are not born at all.

B)
āgacchanto] MS: āganto

VI

gal te de'i las kyis der
'byung ba dag ni 'byung ba dang |
de bzhin 'gyur bar 'dug na go |
rnam par shes par cis mi 'dod || [6]

D) de'i las rnams kyis der rnam par shes pa nyid der de lta bur 'gyur ba ci'i phyir mi 'dod la | E) ci'i phyir 'byung ba rnams su rtog |

VI

yadi tatkarmmabhis tatra bhūtānāṁ sambhavas tathā |
iṣyate pariṇāmaś ca kiṁ vijñānasya neṣyate || *6* ||

D) (*vi*)**jñā**nasyaiva tatkarmmabhis tathāpariṇāmaḥ kasmān neṣyate ⟨ | ⟩ E) kim punar bhūtāni kalpyante || F) api ca ||

[Vasubandhu]

If you accept that gross material elements arise there in
this fashion through the karmic deeds of those [beings],
And [you accept their] transformation, why do you not
accept [the transformation] of cognition? [6]

D) Why do you not accept that the transformation thus brought about by the karmic deeds of those [beings] is [a transformation] of cognition itself? E) Why, moreover, are gross material elements imagined [to play any role at all]? F) What is more:

VII

gzhan na las kyi bag chags la ||
'bras bu dag ni gzhan du rtog ||
gang na bag chags yod pa der ||
ci'i phyir na 'dod mi bya || [7]

A) sems can dmyal ba pa rnams kyi las gang gis der 'byung ba dag de lta bur 'byung ba dang | 'gyur bar yang rtog pa'i las de'i bag chags de dag nyid kyi rnam par shes pa'i rgyud la gnas te | gzhan ma yin na B) bag chags de gang na yod pa de dag nyid la de'i 'bras bu rnam par shes par gyur pa de 'dra bar ci'i phyir mi 'dod la | C) gang na bag chags med pa der de'i 'bras bu rtog ba 'di la gtan tshigs ci yod |

VII

karmmaṇo vāsanānyatra phalam anyatra kalpyate |
tatraiva neṣyate **ya**tra vāsanā kin nu kāraṇaṁ || 7 ||

A) yena hi karmmaṇā nārakāṇāṁ tatra tādṛśo bhūtānāṁ sambhavaḥ kalpyate pariṇāmaś ca tasya karmmaṇo vāsanā teṣāṁ vi[jñā]na(*saṁtāna*)**sa**nniviṣṭā nānyatra , B) yatraiva ca vāsanā tatraiva tasyāḥ phalaṁ tādṛśo vijñānapariṇāmaḥ kin neṣyate ⟨ | ⟩ C) yatra vāsanā nāsti tatra tasyāḥ phalaṁ kalpyata iti kim a(*t*)ra **kāra**ṇaṁ |

The perfuming of the karmic deed you imagine to be elsewhere than the result;
What is the reason you do not accept [that the result is] in precisely the same location where the perfuming [takes place]? [7]

A) You imagine such an arising and transformation of gross material elements of hell beings there [in hell] as due to their karmic deeds, while the perfuming of those karmic deeds is lodged in their individual continua of cognition, not elsewhere. B) So why do you not accept that such a transformation of cognition as the result of those [karmic deeds] is precisely where the perfuming itself is? C) For what reason, in this case, do you imagine that the result of those [karmic deeds] is somewhere where the perfuming is not?

VII

D) smras pa | lung gi gtan tshigs yod de | E) gal te rnam par shes pa nyid gzugs la sogs par snang gi | gzugs la sogs pa'i don ni med na gzugs la sogs pa'i skye mched yod par ni bcom ldan 'das kyis gsung bar mi 'gyur ro zhe na |

VII

D) āgamaḥ kāraṇaṁ | E) yadi vijñānam eva rūpādipratibhāsaṁ syān na rūpādiko ⟨'⟩rthas tadā rūpādyāyatanāstitvaṁ bhagavatā noktaṁ syāt* |

[Objection]

D) The reason is scripture. E) If there were nothing but cognition with the appearance of material form and the rest, and no external objects characterized as material form and the rest, then the Blessed One would not have spoken of the existence of the sense-fields of material form and the rest.

VIII

A) 'di ni gtan tshigs ma yin te | 'di ltar |

gzugs sogs skye mched yod par ni ||
des 'dul ba yi skye bo la ||
dgongs pa'i dbang gis gsungs pa ste ||
rdzus te byung ba'i sems can bzhin || [8]

B) dper na bcom ldan 'das kyis rdzus te byung ba'i sems can bzhin yod do || zhes gsungs pa yang phyi ma la sems kyi rgyud rgyun mi 'chad pa la dgongs nas dgongs pa'i dbang gis gsungs pa ste |

VIII

A) akāraṇam etat* yasmāt* ,

rūpādyāyatanāstitvaṁ tadvineyajanam prati |
abhiprāyavaśād uktam upapādukasatvavat* || [8 ||]

B) yathāsti satva upapāduka ity uktaṁ bhagavatā 'bhiprāyavaśāc cittasantatyanucchedam ā<3b1>yatyām abhipretya |

[Vasubandhu]

A) This is not a reason, since:

The existence of the sense-fields of material form and the rest were spoken of [by the Blessed One] with a special intention directed toward the individual to be guided by that [teaching], as [in the case of the mention of] beings born by spontaneous generation. [8]

B) By way of example, the Blessed One with a special intention said "There are beings of spontaneous birth," intending [allusion to] the nonannihilation of the continuum of mind in the future. D) [We know this] because of the [scriptural] statement:

VIII

C) 'di na bdag gam sems can med ||
chos 'di rgyu dang bcas las byung ||

D) zhes gsungs pa'i phyir ro || E) de bzhin du bcom ldan 'das kyis gzugs la sogs pa'i skye mched yod par gsungs pa yang de bstan pas 'dul ba'i skye bo'i ched du ste | bka' de ni dgongs pa can no ||

VIII

C) nāstīha satva ātmā vā dharmmās tv ete sahetukāḥ ⟨ || ⟩

D) iti vacanāt* | E) evaṁ rūpādyāyatanāstitvam apy uktaṁ bhagavatā taddeśanāvineyajanam adhikṛtyety ābhiprāyikaṁ tad vacanaṁ |

C) Here [in our teaching] there is no being or self,
but [only] these elemental factors of existence along with their causes.

E) Thus, although the Blessed One did speak of the existence of the sense-fields of form and the rest, that [scriptural] statement is of special intention since it is directed toward the individual who is to be guided by that teaching.

IX

A) ’dir ci las dgongs she na |

rang gi sa bon gang las su ||
rnam rig snang ba gang byung ba ||
de dag de yi skye mched ni ||
rnam pa gnyis su thub pas gsungs || [9]

IX

A) ko ⟨'⟩trābhiprāyaḥ |

yataḥ svabījād vijñaptir yadābhāsā pravarttate |
dvividhāyatanatvena te tasyā munir abravīt* || [9 ||]

A) In this regard, what is the special intention?

A manifestation arises from its own proper seed, having an appearance corresponding to that [external object]. The Sage spoke of the two [seed and appearance] as the dual sense field of that [manifestation]. [9]

IX

B) 'di skad du bstan par 'gyur zhe na | C) gzugs su snang ba'i rnam par rig pa rang gi sa bon 'gyur ba'i bye brag tu gyur pa gang las byung ba'i sa bon de dang | snang ba gang yin pa D) de dang de dag ni de'i mig dang | gzugs kyi skye mched du bcom ldan 'das kyis go rims bzhin du gsungs so || E) de bzhin du reg byar snang ba'i rnam par rig pa'i bar du rang rang gi sa bon 'gyur ba'i bye brag tu gyur pa'i sa bon gang las byung ba'i sa bon de dang | snang ba gang yin pa F) de dang de dag ni bcom ldan 'das kyis de'i lus dang reg bya'i skye mched du go rims bzhin du gsungs te | G) 'di ni 'dir dgongs pa'o ||

IX

B) kim uktam bhavati | C) rūpapratibhāsā vijñaptir yataḥ svabījāt pariṇāmaviśeṣaprāptād utpadyate tac ca bījaṁ yatpratibhāsā ca D) sā te tasyā vijñapteś cakṣūrūpāyatanatvena yathākramaṁ bhagavān abravīt* | E) evaṁ yāvat spraṣṭavyapratibhā**sā** vijñaptir yataḥ svabījāt pariṇāmaviśeṣaprāptād utpadyate , tac ca bījaṁ yatpratibhāsā ca F) sā te tasyāḥ kāyaspraṣṭavyāyatanatvena yathākramam bhagavān abravīd G) ity aya[m] (*abhi*)**prā**yaḥ |

B) What is being stated? C) The proper seed from which—when it has attained a particular transformation—arises a manifestation having the appearance of visible form, and that as which this [cognition] appears: D) the Blessed One spoke of these two as, respectively, the sense field of visual perception ["seeing eye" = seed] and the sense field of visible form [= the object] related to that manifestation. E) The same [applies to all items in the stock list] up to: The Blessed One spoke of the proper seed from which—when it has attained a particular transformation—arises a manifestation having the appearance of the tangible, and that as which this [manifestation] appears: F) [the Blessed One spoke] of these two as, respectively, the sense field of tangible perception ["body" = seed] and the sense field of the tangible [= the object] related to that [manifestation]. G) This is the special intention.

E)
pariṇāmaviśeṣaprāptād] MS: pariṇāmaviśeṣād

X

A) de ltar dgongs pa'i dbang gis bstan pa la yon tan ci yod ce na |

de ltar gang zag la bdag med par
'jug par 'gyur ro || [10ab]

B) de ltar bshad na gang zag la bdag med par 'jug par 'gyur te | C) drug po gnyis las rnam par shes pa drug 'byung gi | lta ba po gcig pu nas reg pa po'i bar du gang yang med par rig nas gang dag gang zag la bdag med par bstan pas 'dul ba de dag gang zag la bdag med par 'jug go|

X

A) evaṁ punar abhiprāyavaśena deśayitvā ko guṇaḥ ||

tathā pudgalanairātmyapraveśo hi ||

B) tathā hi deśyamāne pudgalanairātmyaṁ praviśanti | C) dva(*ya*)ṣ[a](*ṭkābhyāṁ vijñā*)**na**ṣaṭkaṁpravarttate na tu kaścid eko draṣṭāsti na yāvan mantety evaṁ viditvā ye pudgalanairātmyadeśanā-vineyās te pudgalanairātmyaṁ praviśanti ||

[Objection]

A) And what is the advantage of having explained things in this way by recourse to special intention?

[Vasubandhu]

For in this way there is understanding of the selflessness of persons. [10ab]

B) For when it is being taught in this way [those individuals to be guided] understand the idea of the selflessness of persons. C) The six cognitions come about from the two sets of six [= the twelve sense-fields], but when they understand that there is no distinct seer at all—[and all members of the stock list] up to—no distinct thinker, those who are to be guided by the teaching of the selflessness of persons understand the idea of the selflessness of persons.

X

gzhan du yang |
bstan pa'i chos la bdag med par
'jug 'gyur || [10bcd]

D) gzhan du yang zhes bya ba ni rnam par rig pa tsam du bstan pa'o || E) ji ltar chos la bdag med par 'jug ce na | F) rnam par rig pa tsam 'di nyid gzugs la sogs pa'i chos su snang bar 'byung ste | G) gzugs la sogs pa'i mtshan nyid kyi chos gang yang med par rig nas 'jug go ||

X

anyathā punar
deśanā dharmanairātmyapraveśaḥ ||

D) anyatheti vijñaptimātradeśanā | E) kathaṁ dharmmanairātmyapraveśaḥ | F) vijñaptimātram idaṁ rūpādidharmmapratibhāsam utpadyate G) na tu rūpādilakṣaṇo dharmma(*ḥ kaścid astī*)<4a1>**ti** viditvā |

Moreover, teaching in another way leads to the understanding of the selflessness of elemental factors of existence. [10bcd]

D) "In another way" refers to the teaching of Manifestation-Only. E) How does this lead to understanding the selflessness of elemental factors of existence? F) [One understands this by] knowing that this Manifestation-Only arises with the semblance of elemental factors of existence such as material form and the rest, G) but actually there is no existing elemental factor of existence having as its characteristic mark material form and the rest.

X

H) gal te chos rnam pa thams cad du med na rnam par rig pa tsam zhes bya ba de yang med pas de ji ltar rnam par gzhag ce na |

X

H) yadi tarhi sarvathā dharmmo nāsti tad api vijñaptimātraṁ nāstīti 〈 | 〉 kathaṁ tarhi vyavasthāpyate |

[Objection]

H) If, then, no elemental factor of existence exists in any fashion, Manifestation-Only does not exist either. How, then, could [your position] be established?

X

1) chos ni rnam pa thams cad du med pa ma yin pas de ltar chos la bdag med par 'jug par 'gyur te |

brtags pa'i bdag nyid kyis | [10d]

X

I) na khalu sarvathā dharmmo nāstīty evaṁ dharmmanairātmyapraveśo bhavati (| J) *a*)pi tu |

kalpitātmanā , [| 10 ||]

[Vasubandhu]

I) It is not the case that one comes to understand the selflessness of elemental factors of existence by thinking that the elemental factors of existence do not exist in any fashion at all. J) But rather [such understanding comes in thinking that elemental factors of existence exist only]:

In terms of an imagined self. [10d]

X

K) gang byis pa rnams kyis chos rnams kyi rang bzhin kun brtags pa'i bdag nyid des de dag bdag med kyi L) sangs rgyas kyi yul gang yin pa brjod du med pa'i bdag nyid kyis ni med pa ma yin no || M) de ltar rnam par rig pa tsam yang rnam par rig pa gzhan gyis kun brtags pa'i bdag nyid kyis bdag med par rtogs pa'i phyir rnam par rig pa tsam du rnam par gzhag pas chos thams cad la chos la bdag med par 'jug pa yin gyi | yod pa de la yang rnam pa thams cad du skur pas ni ma yin no || N) gzhan du na ni rnam par rig pa gzhan yang rnam par rig pa gzhan gyi don du 'gyur bas rnam par rig pa tsam nyid du mi 'grub ste | rnam par rig pa rnams don dang ldan pa'i phyir ro ||

X

K) yo bālair dharmāṇāṁ svabhāvo grāhyagrāhakādiḥ parikalpitas tena kalpitenātmanā teṣāṁ nairātmyaṁ L) na tv anabhilāpyenātmanā yo buddhānām viṣaya iti | M) evam vijña[pti](*mātrasyā*)**pi** vijñaptyantaraparikalpitenātmanā nairātmyapraveśād vijñaptimātravyavasthāpanayā sarvadharmmāṇāṁ nairātmyapraveśo bhavati na tu sarvathā tada(*s*)t(*i*)tvāpavād(*ā*)**t*** | N) itarathā hi vijñapter api vijñaptyantaram arthaḥ syād iti vijñaptimātratvan na sidhyetārthavatītvād vijñaptīnāṁ |

K) The reference is to the selflessness of those elemental factors of existence the intrinsic nature of which—characterized by subject and object and so on—fools fantasize in terms of an imagined self. L) [The reference] is not to [the selflessness of elemental factors of existence] in terms of the inexpressible self, which is the domain of the Buddhas. M) In this way, Manifestation-Only also leads to an understanding of the selflessness of all elemental factors of existence through the establishment of the fact of Manifestation-Only because of an understanding of selflessness in terms of a self fantasized by another manifestation, not because of a denial of the existence of those [elemental factors of existence] in each and every respect. N) For otherwise one manifestation would have another manifestation as its external object, and therefore the fact of Manifestation-Only could not be proved, because manifestations would possess external objects.

M)
nairātmyapraveśād] MS: nairātmyapraveśā

XI

A) bcom ldan 'das kyis dgongs pa 'dis gzugs la sogs pa'i skye mched yod par gsungs kyi | gzugs la sogs pa gang dag yod bzhin du de dag rnam par rig pa so so'i yul du mi 'gyur ro zhes bya ba de ji ltar rtogs par bya zhe na |

XI

A) kathaṁ punar idaṁ pratyetavyam anenābhiprāyeṇa bhagavatā rūpādyāyatanāstitvam uktaṁ na punaḥ santy eva tāni yāni rūpādivijñaptīnāṁ pratyekaṁ viṣayībhavantīti |

[Objection]

A) How, then, should one understand this, namely, that while the Blessed One spoke of the existence of the sense-fields of visible form and the rest with this special intention, those things which come to be the corresponding sense objects of the manifestations of visible form and the rest do not actually exist at all?

XI

B) 'di ltar |

de ni gcig na'ang yul min la ||
phra rab rdul du du ma'ang min ||
de dag 'dus pa 'ang ma yin te ||
'di ltar rdul phran mi 'grub phyir || [11]

XI

B) yasmān

na tad ekaṁ na cānekaṁ viṣayaḥ paramāṇuśaḥ |
na ca te saṁhatā yasmāt paramāṇur na sidhyati || [11 ||]

[Vasubandhu]

B) Since:

That [sense-field of form and the rest] is not a unitary nor atomically plural sense object, neither are those [atoms] compounded, since the atom [itself] is not proved. [11]

XI

C) ji skad du bstan par 'gyur zhe na | D) gang gzugs la sogs pa'i skye mched gzugs la sogs pa rnam par rig pa so so'i yul yin du zin na de ni gcig pu zhig yin te | ji ltar bye brag pa rnams kyis cha shas can gyi ngo bor brtag pa'i lta bu 'am | rdul phra rab du ma 'am rdul phra rab de dag nyid 'dus pa zhig tu 'gyur grang na | E) gcig pu de ni yul ma yin te | cha shas rnams las gzhan pa cha shas can gyi ngo bo gang la'ang mi 'dzin pa'i phyir ro || F) du ma'ang yul ma yin te | rdul phra rab so so la mi 'dzin pa'i phyir ro || G) de dag 'dus pa yang yul ma yin te | 'di ltar rdul phra rab rdzas gcig tu mi 'grub pa'i phyir ro ||

XI

C) iti ⟨ | ⟩ kim uktam bhavati | D) yat tad rūpādikam āyatanaṁ rūpādivijñaptīnāṁ pratyekaṁ viṣayaḥ syāt tad ekaṁ vā syād yathā 'vayavirū**paṁ** kalpyate vaiśeṣikaiḥ anekaṁ vā paramāṇuśaḥ saṁhatā vā ta eva paramāṇavaḥ | E) na tāvad ekaṁ viṣayo bhavaty avayavebhyo ⟨'⟩nyasyāvayavirūpasya kvacid apy agrahaṇāt* | F) nāpy anekaṁ <4b1> **pa**ramāṇūnāṁ pratyekam agrahaṇāt* | G) nāpi te saṁhatā viṣayībhavanti | yasmāt paramāṇur ekaṁ dravyaṁ na sidhyati |

C) What is stated here? D) Whatever sense-field, consisting of visible form and the rest, would be the corresponding sense object of the manifestations of visible form and the rest, would be either unitary—as the Vaiśeṣikas imagine material form as a part-possessing whole—or it would be atomically plural, or it would be compounded of those very atoms themselves. E) First of all, the sense object is not unitary, because there is no apprehension anywhere at all of a material form as a part-possessing whole separate from its parts. F) Nor is it plural, because there is no apprehension of atoms individually. G) Nor would those [atoms], compounded, come to be the sense object, since the atom is not proved to be a singular substance.

XII

A) ji ltar mi 'grub ce na |

B) 'di ltar ||

> drug gis cig car sbyar bas na ||
> phra rab rdul cha drug tu 'gyur || [12ab]

C) phyogs drug nas rdul phra rab drug gis cig car du sbyar na ni rdul phra rab cha drug tu 'gyur te | gcig gi go gang yin pa der gzhan mi 'byung ba'i phyir ro ||

XII

A) kathaṁ na sidhyati |

B) yasmāt* |

ṣaṭkena yugapadyogāt paramāṇoḥ ṣaḍaṅśatā ||

C) ṣaḍ**bhyo** digbhyaḥ ṣaḍbhiḥ paramāṇubhir yugapadyoge sati paramāṇoḥ ṣaḍaṅśatā prāpnoti | ekasya yo deśas tatrānyasyāsambhavāt* |

[Objection]

A) How is [the atom as a singular substance] not proved?

[Vasubandhu]

B) Since:

Because [either] in the simultaneous conjunction with a group of six [other atoms], the atom [would have to] have six parts, [12ab]

C) If there were simultaneous conjunction with six atoms from the six directions [of possible orientation], this would result in the atom having six parts, because where there is one thing another cannot arise.

XII

drug po dag kyang go gcig na ||
gong bu rdul phran tsam du 'gyur || [12cd]

D) ji ste rdul phra rab gcig gi go gang yin pa de nyid du drug po rnams kyi go yang yin na ni E) des na thams cad go gcig pa'i phyir gong bu thams cad rdul phra rab tsam du 'gyur te | phan tshun tha dad pa med pa'i phyir F) gong bu gang yang snang bar mi 'gyur ro || G) kha che'i bye brag tu smra ba rnams nyes pa 'di 'byung du 'ong ngo zhes te | rdul phra rab rnams ni cha shas med pa'i phyir sbyor ba ma yin gyi | 'dus pa dag ni phan tshun sbyor ro zhes zer ba H) de dag la 'di skad du | I) rdul phra rab rnams 'dus pa gang yin pa de de dag las don gzhan rnams ma yin no zhes brjod par bya'o ||

XII

ṣaṇṇāṁ samānadeśatvāt piṇḍaḥ syād aṇumātrakaḥ || [12 ||]

D) atha ya evaikasya paramāṇor deśaḥ sa eva ṣaṇṇāṁ ⟨ | ⟩ E) tena sarveṣāṁ samānadeśatvāt sarvaḥ piṇḍaḥ paramāṇumātraḥ syāt parasparāvyatirekād F) iti na kaścit piṇḍo dr̥śyaḥ syāt* | G) naiva hi paramāṇavaḥ saṁyujyante niravayavatvāt ⟨ | ⟩ mā bhūd eṣa doṣaprasaṅgaḥ ⟨ | ⟩ saṁghātās tu parasparaṁ saṁyujyanta iti kāśmīravaibhāṣikās ⟨ | ⟩ H) te idaṁ praṣṭavyāḥ | I) yaḥ paramāṇūnāṁ saṁghāto na sa tebhyo 'rthāntaram iti ||

[Or] because, the six being in a common location, the cluster would be the extent of a [single] atom. [12cd]

D) Or, the place in which there are six atoms would be precisely the same as the place of the single atom. E) For this [reason], because all of them would be in a common location, the entire cluster would be the extent of a [single] atom, because they would not exclude one another. F) Thus no cluster would be visible at all. G) The Kashmiri Vaibhāṣikas say: "Atoms do not at all conjoin, because of being partless—absolutely not! But compounded things do conjoin one with another." H) They should be questioned as follows: I) Since a compound of atoms is not something separate from those [atoms],

G)
niravayavatvāt] MS: niravayatvāt

XIII

rdul phran sbyor ba med na ni ||
de ’dus yod pa de gang gis || [13ab]

A) sbyor ba zhes bya bar bsnyegs so ||

cha shas yod ba ma yin pas ||
de sbyor mi ’grub ma zer cig | [13cd]

B) ji ste ’dus pa dag kyang phan tshun mi sbyor ro zhe na | rdul phra rab rnams ni cha shas med pa’i phyir sbyor ba mi ’grub bo zhes ma zer cig | ’dus pa cha shas dang bcas pa yang sbyor bar khas mi len pa’i phyir ro || C) de bas rdul phra rab rdzas gcig pu mi ’grub bo || D) rdul phra rab sbyor bar ’dod kyang rung mi ’dod kyang rung ste |

XIII

paramāṇor asaṁyoge tatsaṁghāte ⟨'⟩sti kasya saḥ ||

A) saṁyoga iti varttate |

na cānavayavatvena tatsaṁyogo na si**dhy**ati || [13 ||]

B) atha saṁghātā apy anyonyaṁ na saṁyujyante na tarhi paramāṇūnāṁ niravayavatvāt saṁyogo na sidhyatīti vaktavyaṁ* | sāvayavasyāpi hi saṁghātasya saṁyogānabhyupa(*gamāt* | C) *ataḥ pa*)**ra**māṇur ekaṁ dravyaṁ na sidhyati | D) yadi ca paramāṇoḥ saṁyoga iṣyate yadi vā neṣyate |

Given that there is no conjunction of atoms, what is [conjoining] when those [atoms] are compounded? [13ab]

A) "Conjoining" is carried over [from the previous].

But it is also not due to their partlessness that the conjunction of those [atoms] is not proved. [13cd]

B) If you now were to claim that even compounds do not conjoin with one another, then you [Kashmiri Vaibhāṣikas] should not say that the conjunction of atoms is not proved because of their partlessness, for a conjunction of the compounded, even with parts, is not admitted. C) Therefore, the atom is not proved as a singular substance. D) And whether a conjunction of atoms is accepted or not:

B)
niravayavatvāt] MS: niravayatvāt

XIV

gang la phyogs cha tha dad yod ||
de ni gcig tu mi rung ngo || [14ab]

A) rdul phra rab kyi shar phyogs kyi cha yang gzhan pa nas 'og gi cha'i bar du yang gzhan te | phyogs kyi cha tha dad na de'i bdag nyid kyi rdul phra rab gcig pur ji ltar rung |

grib dang sgrib par ji ltar 'gyur || [14c]

XIV

digbhāgabhedo yasyāsti tasyaikatvan na yujyate |

A) anyo hi paramāṇoḥ [p]ū(*rvadig*)[bh](*āgo*) <5a1> yāvad adhodigbhāga iti digbhāgabhede sati kathaṁ tadātmakasya paramāṇor ekatvaṁ yokṣyate |

chāyāvṛtī kathaṁ vā |

It is not reasonable that something with spatial differentiation be singular. [14ab]

A) If there were spatial differentiation of an atom—namely, the front part is different [and so are all the other sides] including the bottom part—how would the singularity of an atom with that [multiple] nature be reasonable?

Or how is there shadow and obstruction? [14c]

XIV

B) gal te rdul phra rab re re la phyogs kyi cha tha dad pa med na ni nyi ma shar ba'i tshe ngos gzhan na ni grib ma 'bab par ji ltar 'gyur te | C) de la ni gang du nyi ma mi 'bab pa'i phyogs gzhan med do || D) gal te phyogs kyi cha tha dad par mi 'dod na rdul phra rab la rdul phra rab gzhan gyis sgrib par yang ji ltar 'gyur | E) rdul phra rab gang la yang cha shas gzhan med na gang du 'ong ba'i phyogs la gcig la gcig thogs par 'gyur | F) thogs pa med na ni thams cad go gcig tu gyur pas 'dus pa thams cad rdul phra rab tsam du 'gyur te | de ni bshad zin to ||

XIV

B) yady ekaikasya paramāṇor digbhāgabhedo na syād ādityodaye katham anyatra pā(*rśv*)[e] ⟨chāyā⟩ **bha**vaty anyatrātapaḥ | C) na hi tasyānyaḥ pradeśo ⟨'⟩sti yatrātapo na syāt* | D) āvaraṇañ ca kathaṁ bhavati paramāṇoḥ paramāṇvantareṇa yadi digbhāgabhedo ne[ṣya]te | E) na hi kaścid a(*nya*)ḥ parabhāgo ⟨'⟩sti yatrāgamanād anyenānyasya pratighātaḥ syāt* | F) asati ca pratighāte sarveṣāṁ samānadeśatvāt sarvaḥ saṁghātaḥ paramāṇumāt[r]a[ḥ sy]ā[d] i[ty] (*uktaṁ* |)

B) If no single atom were to have spatial differentiation, how is it that when the sun rises in one place, there is shadow in one place, sunshine in another? C) For that [atom] does not have another portion on which there would be no sunshine. D) And how is an atom obstructed by another atom if spatial differentiation is not accepted? E) For [an atom] has no other separate part whatsoever, from contact with which one [atom] would be resisted by another. F) And if there were no resistance, then because all of them would share a common location, the entire compound would be the extent of a [single] atom, as has [already] been discussed [in verse 12cd, above].

XIV

G) grib ma dang sgrib pa rdul phra rab kyi ma yin yang | ci gong bu'i yin pa de ltar yang mi 'dod dam |

H) rdul phra rab rnams las gong bu gzhan zhig yin par 'dod dam ci na de dag de'i yin |

I) smras pa | ma yin no ||

I)
ma yin no] All editions: *yin no*

XIV

G) **kim** evaṁ neṣyate piṇḍasya te cchāyāvṛtī na paramāṇor iti |

H) kiṁ khalu paramāṇubhyo 'nyaḥ piṇḍa iṣyate yasya te syātāṁ ⟨|⟩

I) nety āha |

[Objection]

G) Do you not accept in this way that the two, shadow and obstruction, belong to the cluster, not to the atom?

[Vasubandhu]

H) Do you, for your part, accept that the cluster which would possess those two [shadow and obstruction] is something other than the atoms ?

[Opponent]

I) We say: no.

XIV

gong bu gzhan min de de'i min || [14d]

J) gal te rdul phra rab rnams las gong bu gzhan ma yin na de dag de'i ma yin par grub pa yin no ||

K) yongs su rtogs pa 'di ni gnas pa'i khyad par te | gzugs la sogs pa'i mtshan nyid ni ma bkag na rdul phra rab ce 'am | 'dus ba zhes bsam pa 'dis ci zhig bya zhe na |

XIV

anyo na piṇḍaś cen na tasya te (|| *14* ||

J) *yadi nā*)**nyaḥ** paramāṇubhyaḥ piṇḍa iṣyate na te tasyeti siddham bhavati |

K) sanniveśaparikalpa eṣaḥ ⟨ | ⟩ paramāṇuḥ saṁghāta iti vā kim anayā cintayā ⟨ | ⟩ lakṣaṇan tu rūpā(*dīnāṁ*) **na** pratiṣidhyate |

[Vasubandhu]

If the cluster is not other [than the atoms], the two [shadow and obstruction] would not be [properties] of that [cluster]. [14cd]

J) If you do not accept the cluster as something other than the atoms, then it is proved that the two [shadow and obstruction] are not [properties] of that [cluster].

[Objection]

K) This is mere imaginative speculation about construction. Why do you have this worry about whether it is an atom or a compound? In any case, the characteristic of visible form and the rest is not negated.

XIV

L) de dag gi mtshan nyid gang yin |

M) mig la sogs pa'i yul nyid dang || sngon po la sogs pa nyid do ||

N) gang mig la sogs pa'i yul sngon po dang | ser po la sogs ba 'dod pa de ci rdzas gcig pu zhig gam | 'on te du ma zhig ces de dpyad par bya'o ||

XIV

L) kim punas teṣāṁ lakṣaṇaṁ

M) cakṣurādiviṣayatvaṁ nīlāditvañ ca

N) tad evedaṁ sampradhāryate ⟨ | ⟩ yat tac cakṣurādīnāṁ viṣayo nīlapītādikam iṣyate kin tad ekaṁ dravyam (*atha vā ta*)**d** anekam iti |

[Vasubandhu]

L) Then what *is* their characteristic?

[Objection]

M) Being a sense-field of visual perception and the rest, and blueness and the like [are the characteristic of visible form].

[Vasubandhu]

N) This is precisely what is being determined: is the sense-field of visual perception and the rest you accept as blue, yellow and so on a single substance, or rather multiple?

XV

A) ’dis ci zhig bya zhe na |

B) du ma’i nyes pa ni bshad zin to ||

gcig na rim gyis ’gro ba med ||
zin dang ma zin cig car med ||
ris chad du mar gnas pa dang ||
mig gis mi sod phra ba ’ang med || [15]

B)
nyes pa] All editions: *nges pa*

XV

A) kiñ cātaḥ |

B) anekatve doṣa uktaḥ ||

ekatve na krameṇetir yugapan na grahāgrahau |
vicchinnānekavṛttiś ca sūkṣmānīkṣā ca no bhavet* || [15 ||]

[Objection]

A) And what [follows] from this?

[Vasubandhu]

B) The fault if it is [judged to be] multiple has already been discussed.

If [the sense object] were singular, there would be no gradual motion, no simultaneous apprehension and non-apprehension, nor divided multiple existence, nor the invisible microscopic. [15]

XV

C) gal te mig gi yul sngon po dang ser po la sogs pa gang yin pa de ris su ma chad de rdzas gcig par rtogs nas la rim gyis ’gro bar mi ’gyur te | gom pa gcig bor bas thams cad du son pa’i phyir ro || D) tshu rol gyi cha zin la pha rol gyi cha ma zin pa cig car du mi ’gyur te | de’i tshe zin pa dang ma zin pa de mi rigs so ||

XV

C) yadi yāvad avicchinnaṁ n[ī](*lādi*)<5b1>**kañ** cakṣuṣo viṣayas tad ekaṁ dravyaṁ kalpyate pṛthivyāṁ krameṇetir na syāt ⟨ | ⟩ gamanam ity arthaḥ | sakṛtpāda(*k*)[ṣ]epeṇa sarvasya gatatvāt* | D) a(*r*)vā[g]-bhā[g]asya ca grahaṇaṁ parabhāgasya cāgra(*haṇaṁ*) **yu**gapan na syāt ⟨ | ⟩ na hi tasyaiva tadānīṁ grahaṇañ cāgrahaṇañ ca yuktam* |

C) If one imagines the visual sense-object, blue and the rest, as long as it is undivided, to be a single substance, there would not be gradual motion on the ground—going, that is to say—because everything would be traversed with a single foot-step. D) And the apprehension of a facing portion and the non-apprehension of the non-facing portion would not be simultaneous, because the apprehension and non-apprehension of the very same thing at that [same] time is not reasonable.

XV

E) glang po che dang rta la sogs pa'i ris su chad pa du ma gcig na 'dug par mi 'gyur te | F) gcig gang na 'dug pa de nyid na gzhan yang 'dug na de dag ris su chad par ji ltar rung | G) de gnyis kyis gang non pa dang ma non pa de dag gcig tu ji ltar rung ste | bar na de dag gis stong pa gzung du yod pa'i phyir ro || H) gal te mtshan nyid tha dad pa nyid kyis rdzas gzhan kho nar rtog gi gzhan du ma yin na go | chu'i skye bo phra mo rnams kyang chen po dag dang gzugs mtshungs pas mig gis mi sod par mi 'gyur ro ||

XV

E) vicchinnasya cānekasya hastyaśvādikasyaikatra vṛttir na syāt ⟨ | ⟩ F) yatraiva hy ekan tatraivāparam iti kathan tayor vicche(*do yujya*)**te** | G) katham vā tad ekaṁ yat prāptañ ca tābhyāṁ na ca prāptam antarāle tacchūnyagrahaṇāt* | H) sūkṣmāṇāñ codakajantūnāṁ sthūlaiḥ samāna-rūpāṇām anīkṣaṇaṁ na syāt* | yadi la(*kṣaṇabhe*)**dād** eva dravyāntara-tvaṁ kalpyate , nānyathā ,

E) And there would be no existence of divided and multiple elephants, horses and so on in a single place; F) because one thing would be just precisely where another is, how could a division between them be reasonable? G) Or on the other hand, how is [it reasonable that] that [place] is single which is [both] occupied by those two [elephant and horse] and not occupied, since one apprehends that the gap between them is empty of the two? H) And, if you were to imagine [the two] to have a difference in substance purely because of a distinction in characteristic feature, not otherwise, microscopic aquatic creatures, having forms like macroscopic [creatures], would not be invisible.

E)
hastyaśvādikasyaikatra] MS: hastyaśvādikasyān ekatra
G)
tad ekaṁ] MS: tadaikaṁ

XV

I) de'i phyir nges par rdul phra rab tha dad par brtag par bya ste | J) de dag gcig tu mi 'grub bo || K) de ma grub pas gzugs la sogs pa yang mig la sogs pa'i yul nyid du mi 'grub ste | L) rnam par rig pa tsam du grub pa yin no ||

XV

I) tasmād avaśyaṁ paramāṇuśo bhedaḥ kalpayitavyaḥ ⟨ | ⟩ J) sa caiko na sidhyati | K) tasyāsiddhau rūpādīnāṁ cakṣ(*u*)rādiviṣayatva(*m asiddham* L) *i*)**ti** siddhaṁ* vijñaptimātram bhavatīti |

I) Therefore [since this is not the case], one must certainly imagine a distinction atomically. J) And that [atom] is not proved to be singular. K) Since [the singular atom] is not proven, the fact that visible form—and the rest—are sense-fields of the visual—and the rest—is unproven; L) therefore Manifestation-Only comes to be proved.

I)
avaśyaṁ] MS: avavaśyaṁ

XVI

A) tshad ma'i dbang gis na yod dam med pa dmigs kyis dbye bar 'gyur la | tshad ma thams cad kyi nang na mngon sum gyi tshad ma ni mchog yin no || B) don de med na 'di ni bdag gi mngon sum mo snyam pa blo 'di ji ltar 'byung zhe na |

XVI

A) pramāṇavaśād astitvaṁ nāstitvaṁ vā nirddhāryate ⟨ | ⟩ sarveṣāñ ca pramāṇānāṁ pratyakṣam pramāṇaṁ gariṣṭham B) ity asaty arthe ka(*tham*) iyaṁ buddhir bha(*vatīdaṁ me*) **pra**tyakṣam iti ||

[Objection]

A) Existence or non-existence is settled on the strength of the valid means of cognition, and of all valid means of cognition, direct perception is the most important valid means of cognition. B) Therefore, if an external object does not exist, how does this awareness come about, namely 'this is before my eyes'?

A)
pramāṇānāṁ] MS: praṇānāṁ

XVI

mngon sum blo ni rmi sogs bzhin || [16a]

C) don med par yang zhes sngar bstan pa nyid do ||

de yang gang tshe de yi tshe ||
khyod kyi don de mi snang na ||
de ni mngon sum ji ltar 'dod || [16bcd]

D) gang gi tshe yul 'di nyid ni bdag gi mngon sum mo snyam du mngon sum gyi blo de byung ba de'i tshe khyod kyi don de mi snang ste | yid kyi rnam par shes pas yongs su bcad pa dang | mig gi rnam par shes pa yang de'i tshe 'gags pa'i phyir ro || EF) lhag par yang skad cig mar smra bas de mngon sum du ji ltar 'dod || de ltar na de'i tshe gzugs dang rol sogs pa de dag ni 'gags zin to ||

XVI

pratyakṣabuddhiḥ svapnādau yathā |

C) vināpy artheneti pūrvam eva jñāpitaṁ* |

sā ca yadā tadā |
na so ⟨'⟩rtho dr̥śyate tasya pratyakṣatvaṁ kathaṁ mataṁ* ||
[16 ||]

[Vasubandhu]

The idea that there is direct perception [of the external object takes place] as in a dream and so on. [16ab]

C) I already earlier made the point that "Even without an external object" [is understood].

Additionally, that external object is not seen [at the moment] when one has [the idea that there is direct perception of an external object]; [so] how can you consider that [the external object] is directly perceived? [16bcd]

XVI

D) gang gi tshe yul 'di nyid ni bdag gi mngon sum mo snyam du mngon sum gyi blo de byung ba de'i tshe khyod kyi don de mi snang ste | yid kyi rnam par shes pas yongs su bcad pa dang | mig gi rnam par shes pa yang de'i tshe 'gags pa'i phyir ro || EF) lhag par yang skad cig mar smra bas de mngon sum du ji ltar 'dod || de ltar na de'i tshe gzugs dang rol sogs pa de dag ni 'gags zin to ||

XVI

D) yad(*ā*) ca sā pratyakṣa(*buddhir bhava*)**tī**daṁ me pratyakṣam iti tadā na so ⟨'⟩rtho dr̥śyate manovijñānenaiva paricchedāc cakṣurvijñānasya ca tadā niruddhatvād E) iti kathaṁ tasya pratyakṣatvam iṣṭaṁ | F) vi[ś]eṣ[e]ṇa tu kṣaṇika(*vādino*) <6a1>**yasya** tadānīṁ niruddham eva tad rūpaṁ rasādikaṁ vā |

D) And [at the moment] when that idea [that there is] direct perception [of the external object] comes about with the thought "This is my direct perception," that external object is not seen [at that same moment], because the discerning takes place only by means of mental cognition, and because at that time the visual cognition [which precedes the mental cognition] has ceased. E) Given this, how can you accept that that [object] is directly perceived? F) What is more, [this holds] especially for one who advocates the momentariness [of all things], for whom [the respective] visible form, or flavor and the rest, has [already] entirely ceased at that time.

XVII

A) myong ba med par yid kyi rnam par shes pa dran par mi 'gyur bas B) don gdon mi za bar myong bar 'gyur te | de ni de mthong ba yin no || C) de ltar de'i yul gzugs la sogs pa mngon sum du 'dod do zhe na |

XVII

A) nānanubhūtam manovijñānena smaryate 〈 | 〉 B) ity avaśyam arthānubhavena bhavitavyaṁ tac ca darśanam ity C) evaṁ tadviṣayasya rūpāde(*ḥ*) p(*r*)atyakṣa**tvaṁ** mataṁ |

[Objection]

A) What was not [previously] experienced cannot be recollected by mental cognition. B) Therefore, there must be experience of an external object, and that is spoken of as 'seeing'. C) In this way I consider it to be a case of an direct perception of that sense-object, [namely] material form and the rest.

XVII

D) myong ba ni don dran pa yin no || zhes de ma grub ste | 'di ltar |

dper na der snang rnam rig bzhin ||
bshad zin | [17ab]

E) dper na don med par don du snang ba mig gi rnam par shes pa la sogs pa'i rnam par rig pa 'byung ba de bzhin te bshad zin to ||

de las dran par zad | [17b]

XVII

D) asiddham idam anubhūtasyārthasya smaraṇam bhavatīti | yasmāt* |

uktaṁ yathā tadābhāsā vijñaptiḥ ||

E) vināpy arthena yathārthābhāsā cakṣurvijñānādikā vijñaptir utpa(*dya*)te ta**tho**ktaṁ ||

smaraṇaṁ tataḥ |

[Vasubandhu]

D) This [argument about] recollection [being] of an experienced external object is unproved, since:

As I discussed, manifestation has the appearance of that [external object]. [17ab]

E) I have discussed how, even in the absence of an external object, a manifestation consisting of visual cognition and so forth arises with the appearance of an external object.

Recollection [comes] from that. [17b]

XVII

F) rnam par rig pa de las dran pa dang mtshungs par ldan pa der snang ba nyid gzugs la sogs pa la rnam par rtog pa yid kyi rnam par rig pa 'byung ste | G) dran pa byung ba las don myong bar mi 'grub bo ||

H) dper na rmi lam gyi rnam par rig pa'i yul yod pa ma yin pa de bzhin du | gal te gnyid kyis ma log pa'i tshe na yang I) de ltar yin na ni de kho na bzhin du de med par 'jig rten rang rang gis khong du chud pa'i rigs na | J) de ltar yang ma yin te | K) de'i phyir rmi lam bzhin du don dmigs pa thams cad don med pa ma yin no zhe na |

XVII

F) tato hi vijñapteḥ smr̥tisamprayuktā tatpratibhāsaiva rūpādivikalpikā manovijñaptir utpadyata G) iti na smr̥tyutpādād arthānubhavaḥ si**dhya**ti |

H) yadi yathā svapne vijñaptir abhūtārthaviṣayā tathā jāgrato ⟨'⟩pi syāt I) tathaiva tadabhāvaṁ lokaḥ svayam avagacchet* ⟨ | ⟩ J) na caivam bhavati ⟨ | ⟩ K) tasmān na svapna ivārthopala**bdhi**ḥ sarvā nirarthikā |

F) For from that manifestation arises a mental manifestation associated with memory, which has precisely the appearance of that [material form] and conceptually fantasizes itself [to refer to] material form and so on; G) thus the arisal of a memory does not prove the experience of an external object.

[Objection]

H) If a manifestation were to have as its sense-object an unreal external object also for one awake, just as is the case in a dream, I) in precisely that way everyone would understand by themselves the nonexistence of that [external object]. J) But that is not how it is. K) Therefore, it is not so that all referential objectifications of external objects are, as is the case in a dream, [actually] devoid of external objects.

XVII

L) de ni gtan tshigs su mi rung ste | 'di ltar |

> rmi lam mthong ba yul med par ||
> ma sad bar du rtogs ma yin || [17cd]

M) de ltar log par rnam par rtog pa la goms pa'i bag chags kyi gnyid kyis log pa'i 'jig rten ni rmi lam bzhin du yang dag pa ma yin pa'i don mthong te | N) ma sad kyi bar du de med par ji lta ba bzhin du rtogs pa ma yin gyi | O) gang gi tshe de'i gnyen po 'jig rten las 'das pa rnam par mi rtog pa'i ye shes thob nas sad par gyur pa de'i tshe de'i rjes las thob pa dag pa 'jig rten pa'i ye shes de mngon du gyur nas yul med par ji lta ba bzhin du khong du chud de de ni mtshungs so ||

XVII

L) idam ajñāpakaṁ* | yasmāt* |

svapnadr̥gviṣayābhāvaṁ nāprabuddho 'vagacchati |[| 17 ||]

M) evaṁ vitathavikalpābhyāsavāsanānidrayā prasupto lokaḥ svapna ivābhūtam artham paśyann N) aprabuddhas tadabhāvaṁ yathāvan nāvagacchati , O) yadā tu tatpratipakṣalokottaranirvikalpa-jñānalābhāt prabuddho bhavati tadā tatpr̥ṣṭhalabdhaśuddhalaukika-jñānasammukhībhāvād viṣayābhāvaṁ yathāvad avagacchatīti samānam etat* |

[Vasubandhu]

L) You cannot draw a conclusion from this, since:

One who is not awake does not understand the non-existence of a sense-object seen in a dream. [17cd]

M) Just so everyone, asleep with the sleep of repeated perfuming of erroneous conceptual fantasy, sees unreal external objects, as in a dream; N) being unawakened, they do not properly understand the non-existence of the [external object]. O) But when they are awakened through the acquisition of supramundane non-discriminative insight which is the antidote to that [erroneous imagination], then they properly understand the non-existence of the sense-object because the subsequently obtained pure worldly insight becomes present. This [situation] is the same.

XVIII

A) gal te rang gi rgyud gyur pa'i khyad par nyid las sems can rnams kyi don du snang ba'i rnam par rig pa 'byung gi | don gyi khyad par las ma yin na | B) brten pa de dang bshad pa de med pas sdig pa'i grogs po dang | dge ba'i bshes gnyen la brten pa dang | dam pa dang dam pa ma yin pa'i chos mnyan pa las sems can rnams kyis rnam par rig pa nges pa ji ltar 'grub par 'gyur |

XVIII

A) yadi svasantānapariṇāmaviśeṣād eva satvānām arthapratibhāsā vijñaptaya utpadyante nārthaviśe<6b1>ṣāt* | B) tadā ya eṣa pāpakalyāṇamitrasaṁparkāt sadasaddharmmaśravaṇāc ca vijñaptiniyamaḥ satvānāṁ sa kathaṁ [si]dhyati , asati sadasatsaṁparke taddeśanāyāñ ca |

[Objection]

A) If manifestations with the appearance of external objects were to arise for beings only through particular transformations of their own mental continua, not through particular external objects, B) then how is it proved that association with bad or good spiritual guides, and hearing true and false teachings, shape the manifestations of beings, if that association with the good and the bad and that teaching do not [actually] exist?

XVIII

gcig la gcig gi dbang gis na ||
rnam par rig pa phan tshun nges || [18ab]

C) sems can thams cad kyi rnam par rig pa phan tshun gyi dbang gis phan tshun du rnam par rig pa rnams nges par 'gyur te | ci rigs su sbyar ro || D) gcig la gcig ces bya ba ni phan tshun no || E) de'i phyir rgyud gzhan gyi rnam par rig pa'i khyad par las rgyud gzhan la rnam par rig pa'i khyad par 'byung gi don gyi khyad par las ni ma yin no ||

XVIII

anyonyādhipatitvena **vijñaptiniyamo** mithaḥ ||

C) sarveṣāṁ hi satvānām anyonyavijñaptyādhipatyena mitho vijñapter niyamo bhavati yathāyogaṁ | D) mitha iti parasparataḥ | E) ataḥ santānāntaravijñaptiviśeṣāt santānāntare vijñaptiviśeṣa utpadyate nārthaviśeṣāt* |

Mutual shaping of manifestation is due to their influence on each other. [18ab]

C) Because all beings exert an influence on each others' manifestations, there comes to be mutual shaping of manifestation, according to the circumstances. D) "Mutually" means "reciprocally." E) Therefore, a distinct manifestation arises within one mental continuum because of a distinct manifestation within another mental continuum, not because of a distinct external object.

XVIII

F) dper na rmi lam gyi rnam par rig pa'i don med ba bzhin du gal te gnyid kyis ma log pa'i yang de lta na gnyid kyis log pa dang ma log pa na dge ba dang mi dge ba'i las kun tu spyod pa'i 'bras bu phyi ma la 'dod pa dang mi 'dod pa 'dra bar ci'i phyir mi 'gyur |

sems ni gnyid kyis non pas na ||
de phyir rmi dang 'bras mi mtshungs || [18cd]

H) de ni 'dir rgyu yin gyi don yod pa ni ma yin no ||

XVIII

F) yadi yathā svapne nirarthikā vijñaptir evañ jāgrato ⟨'⟩pi syāt kasmāt kuśalākuśalasamudācāre **su**ptāsuptayos tulyaṁ phalam iṣṭāniṣṭam āyatyān na bhavati ⟨ | ⟩

G) yasmāt* |

middhenopahatañ cittaṁ svapne tenāsamaṁ phalaṁ
|[|18 ||]

H) idam atra kāraṇaṁ na tv arthasadbhāvaḥ |

[Objection]

F) If [as you claim] a manifestation were devoid of an external object likewise also for one awake, as is the case in a dream, why do those asleep and those not asleep not come in the future to have the same [karmic] result, desired and undesired [respectively], of [their] wholesome and unwholesome behavior?

[Vasubandhu]

G) Since:

When one dreams, the mind is overpowered by sloth; thus the result is not the same. [18cd]

H) This is the cause in this case, and not [some alleged] real existence of an external object.

XIX

A) gal te 'di dag rnam par rig pa tsam du zad na gang la yang lus dang ngag kyang med pas shan pa la sogs pas gsod pa na lug la sogs pa 'chi bar ji ltar 'gyur | B) 'chi ba de des ma byas na ni shan pa la sogs pa srog gcod pa'i kha na ma tho ba dang ldan par ji ltar 'gyur zhe na |

XIX

A) yadi vijña**pti**mātram evedaṁ na kasyacit kāyo ⟨'⟩sti na vāk* katham upakramyamāṇānām aurabhrikādibhir urabhrādīnāṁ maraṇam bhavati , B) atatkṛte vā tanmaraṇe katham aurabhrikādīnāṁ **prā**ṇātipātāvadyena yogo bhavati ||

[Objection]

A) If this [world] is nothing but Manifestation-Only, and no one has a body or voice, how does the death of rams and others being attacked by butchers come about? B) Or if their death is not due to those [butchers], how does there come to be a connection between the butchers and the crime of taking life?

A)
upakramya°] MS: anukramya°

XIX

'chi ba gzhan gyi rnam rig gi ||
bye brag las de dper bya na ||
'dre la sogs pa'i yid dbang gis ||
gzhan gyi dran nyams 'gyur sogs bzhin || [19]

C) dper na 'dre la sogs pa'i yid kyi dbang gis gzhan dag gi dran pa nyams pa dang | rmi ltas su mthong ba dang | 'byung po'i gdon phab par 'gyur ba dang | D) rdzu 'phrul dang ldan pa'i yid kyi dbang gis te | E) dper na 'phags pa kā tyā'i bu chen po'i byin gyi brlabs kyis sa ra ṇas rmi ltas su mthong ba dang | F) drang srong dgon pa pa'i yid 'khrugs pas thags zangs ris G) bzhin du gzhan gyi rnam par rig pa'i bye brag gis sems can gzhan gyi srog gi dbang po dang mi mthun pa'i 'gyur ba 'ga' 'byung ste | des skal ba 'dra ba'i rgyud kyi rgyun chad pa zhes bya ba 'chi bar rig par bya'o ||

G)
skal ba] All editions: *bskal pa*

XIX

maraṇaṁ paravijñaptiviśeṣād vikriyā yathā |
smṛtilopādikānyeṣāṁ piśācādimanovaśāt* || [19 ||]

C) yathā hi piśācādimanovaśād anyeṣāṁ smṛtilopasvapnadarśanabhūtagrahāveśavikārā bhavanti | D) ṛddhivanmanovaśāc ca | E) yathā sāraṇasyāryamahākātyāyanādhiṣṭhānāt svapnadarśanaṁ | F) āraṇyakarṣimanaḥpradoṣāc ca vema[c]itriṇa<7a1>ḥ parājayaḥ | G) tathā paravijñaptiviśeṣādhipatyāt pareṣāṁ jīvitendriyavirodhinī kācid vikriyotpadyate yayā sabhāgasantativicchedākhyam maraṇam bhavatīti veditavyaṁ |

Death is a transformation due to a particular manifestation of another, just as the transformation of memory loss and the like of others is due to the mental force of demons and so on. [19]

C) Just as, due to the mental force of demons and so on others come to experience dislocations [including] memory loss, dream visions and possession by ghouls of illness, D) and [this also takes place] due to the mental force of those possessed of superpowers— E) For example, Sāraṇa had a dream vision due to the controlling power of Ārya-Mahākātyāyana, F) and the conquest of Vemacitrin was due to the hostility of the forest ascetics— G) Just so, it is due to the influence of a particular manifestation of another that there arises some transformation of others obstructing the life force, by which there comes to be death, designated as the cutting off of related [mental] continuities. This is how it should be understood.

XX

drang srong khros pas dan ta ka'i ||
dgon pa ji ltar stongs par 'gyur || [20ab]

A) gal te gzhan gyi rnam par rig pa'i bye brag gis sems can dag 'chi bar mi 'dod na | B) yid kyi nyes pa kha na ma tho ba chen po dang bcas pa nyid du bsgrub pa na | bcom ldan 'das kyis khyim bdag nye ba 'khor la bka' stsal pa | C) khyim bdag khyod kyis dan ta ka'i dgon pa dang | ka ling ka'i dgon pa dang ma tang ka'i dgon pa de dag ci zhig gis stongs pa dang | gtsang mar gyur pa ci thos zhes smras pa dang | D) des gau ta ma drang srong rnams khros pas de ltar gyur ces thos so zhes gsol to ||

XX

katham vā daṇḍakāraṇyaśūnyatvam r̥ṣikopataḥ |

ᴀ) yadi paravijñaptiviśeṣādhipatyāt satvānāṁ maraṇaṁ neṣyate |
ʙ) manodaṇḍasya hi mahāsāvadyatvaṁ sādhayatā bhagavatopālir
gr̥hapatiḥ pr̥ṣṭaḥ c) kaccit te gr̥hapate śrutaṁ kena tāni daṇḍakāraṇyāni
mātaṅgāraṇyāni kaliṅgāraṇyāni śūnyāni medhyībhūtāni ⟨ | ⟩ ᴅ) tenok-
taṁ śrutaṁ me bho gautama r̥ṣīṇāṁ manaḥpradoṣeṇeti ||

**Otherwise, how did the Daṇḍaka forest become emptied by
the sages' anger?** [20ab]

ᴀ) If you do not accept that beings die because of the influence
of a particular manifestation of another [how do you account for what
happened in the Daṇḍaka forests?]. ʙ) For the Blessed One, in proving
that mental violence is highly objectionable, asked the householder
Upāli: c) "Have you heard anything, householder? By whom were the
Daṇḍaka forests, the Mātaṅga forests, and the Kaliṅga forests emptied
and made ritually pure?" ᴇ) He said: "I have heard, O Gautama, it was
through the mental hostility of the sages."

yid nyes kha na ma tho cher ||
ji ltar de yis 'grub par 'gyur || [20cd]

E) gal te 'di ltar rtog ste || de la dga' ba mi ma yin pa de dag gis de na gnas pa'i sems can rnams kha btag gi | drang srong rnams kyis yid 'khrugs pas dogs pa ni ma yin no zhe na | F) de ltar na las des lus dang ngag gi nyes pa rnams pas yid kyi nyes pa ches kha na ma tho ba chen po dang bcas par 'grub par ji ltar 'gyur te | G) de'i yid 'khrugs pa tsam gyis sems can de snyed 'chi bar 'grub bo ||

XX

manodaṇḍo mahāvadyaḥ kathaṁ vā tena sidhyati ||[| 20 ||]

E) yady evaṁ kalpyate , tadabhiprasannair amānuṣais tadvāsinaḥ satvā utsāditā na tv ṛ̥ṣīṇāṁ* **ma**naḥpradoṣān mṛ̥tā ity F) evaṁ sati kathaṁ tena karmmaṇā manodaṇḍaḥ kāyavāgdaṇḍābhyām mahāvadyatamaḥ siddho bhavati 〈 | 〉 G) tan manaḥpradoṣamātreṇa tāvatāṁ satvā**nā**ṁ* maraṇāt sidhyati |

Or how does that prove mental violence is a great violation?

[20cd]

E) If you were to imagine as follows: beings dwelling there were annihilated by non-humans favorable to those [sages], rather than dying due to the mental hostility of the sages— F) if such were the case, how does that action prove mental violence to be a much greater violation than physical or verbal violence? G) That is proved by the death of so many beings solely on account of mental hostility.

XXI

A) gal te ’di dag rnam par rig pa tsam du zad na gzhan gyi sems rig pas ci gzhan gyi sems shes sam ’on te mi shes she na | B) ’dis ci zhig bya | C) gal te mi shes na ni gzhan gyi sems rig pa zhes kyang ci skad du bya | D) ji ste shes na yang |

XXI

A) yadi vijñaptimātram evedaṁ paracittavidaḥ kiṁ paracittaṁ jānanty , atha na , B) kiñ cātaḥ | C) yadi na jānanti kathaṁ paracittavido bhavanti | D) atha jānanti |

[Objection]

A) If this [world] is nothing but Manifestation-Only, do then "those who know other minds" [really] know other minds, or not? B) And what [follows] from this? C) If they do not know, how do they become those who [are spoken of as ones who] know others minds? D) Or they do know [which is only possible if external objects do really exist, in which case]:

XXI

gzhan sems rig pas shes pa ni ||
don bzhin ma yin ji ltar dper ||
rang sems shes pa | [21abc]

E) de yang ji ltar don ji lta ba bzhin du ma yin zhe na |

sangs rgyas kyi
spyod yul ji bzhin ma shes phyir | [21cd]

F) ji ltar de brjod du med pa'i bdag nyid du sangs rgyas kyi spyod yul du gyur pa de ltar des ma shes pa'i phyir de gnyi ga yang don ji lta ba bzhin ma yin te | G) log par snang ba'i phyir ro || H) gzung ba dang 'dzin pa'i rnam par rtog pa ma spangs pa'i phyir ro ||

XXI

paracittavidāṁ jñānam ayathārthaṁ* kathaṁ* yathā ,
svacittajñānaṁ*

E) tad api katham ayathārthaṁ* |

ajñānād yathā buddhasya gocaraḥ || [21 ||]

F) yathā tan nirabhilāpyenātmanā b(*u*)<7b1>**ddhānāṁ** gocaraḥ | tathā tadajñānāt ⟨ | ⟩ tad ubhayaṁ na yathārthaṁ G) vitathapratibhāsatayā H) grāhyagrāhakavikalpasyāprahīṇatvāt* |

How is the knowledge of those who know other minds inconsistent with reality?
[Reply:] **It is as with knowledge of one's own mind.** [21abc]

E) How is that [knowledge of one's own mind] also inconsistent with reality?

Because one does not know [other minds or even one's own] in the way that [such knowing of minds] is the scope of a Buddha. [21cd]

F) Because we do not know that in the way that that [knowledge] is the scope of the buddhas, with respect to its nature as inexpressible. Both [knowledges, of one's own mind and of those of others,] are inconsistent with reality, G) because [all that non-buddhas are able to know is an] erroneous appearance. H) This is because they fail to reject the conceptual fantasy of subject and object.

XXII

A) rnam par rig pa tsam gyis rab tu dbye ba rnam par nges pa mtha' yas la gting mi dpogs shing zab pa'i |

rnam rig tsam du grub pa 'di ||
bdag gis bdag gi mthu 'dra bar ||
byas kyi de yi rnam pa kun ||
bsam yas | [22abcd]

XXII

A) anantaviniścayaprabhedāgādhagāmbhīryāyāṁ vijñaptimātratāyāṁ ⟨ | ⟩

vijñaptimātratāsiddhiḥ svaśaktisadṛśī mayā |
kṛteyaṁ sarvathā sā tu na cintyā ,

A) Because [the idea of] Manifestation-Only has unfathomable depth, its explanations and divisions endless,

I have composed this proof of [the World as] Manifestation-Only according to my ability, but that [fact that the World is nothing but Manifestation-Only] is not conceivable in its entirety. [22abcd]

XXII

B) bdag 'dra bas rnam pa thams cad ni bsam par mi nus te | rtog ge'i spyod yul ma yin pa'i phyir ro || C) 'o na de rnam pa thams cad du su'i spyod yul snyam pa la |

sangs rgyas spyod yul lo [22d]

zhes bya ba smos te | D) de ni sangs rgyas bcom ldan 'das rnams kyi spyod yul te | shes bya thams cad kyi rnam pa thams cad la mkhyen pa thogs pa mi mnga' ba'i phyir ro ||

XXII

B) sarvaprakārā tu sā mādr̥śaiś cintayituṁ na śakyā tarkkāviṣayatvāt* | C) kasya **punaḥ** sā sarvathā gocara ity āha |

buddhagocaraḥ , [| 22 ||]

D) buddhānāṁ hi sā bhagavatāṁ sarvaprakāraṁ gocaraḥ sarvākārasarvajñeyajñānāvighātād iti ||

B) However, that [idea of Manifestation-Only] cannot be conceived in all its aspects by those like me, because it is beyond the domain of logical reasoning. C) For whom, then, is this [idea] in all respects the [proper] scope? We reply:

It is the scope of the buddhas. [22d]

D) For it is the scope of the buddhas, the Blessed Ones, in all aspects, because their knowledge of all objects of knowledge in all ways is unobstructed.

Colophon

slob dpon dbyig gnyen gyis mdzad pa nyi shu ba'i 'grel pa rdzogs so ||

|| rgya gar gyi mkhan po dzi na mi tra dang | shī len dra bo dhi dang | zhu chen gyi lo tsā ba ban de ye shes sdes zhus te gtan la phab pa ||

Colophon

viṁśikā vijñaptimātratāsiddhiḥ
kṛtir iyam ācāryavasubandhoḥ ||

This is the Proof of [the World as] Manifestation-Only in Twenty Verses
A composition of the Master Vasubandhu.

viṁśikā] MS: viṁśatikā

Notes and Commentary

I/II

In his edition, Sylvain Lévi (1925: 3) 'restored' the missing first leaf of the *Viṁśikā* and its autocommentary. Later, Nasu Jisshū (1953: 114) offered a revised version. For these, see below. While most of the reconstructions remain unverifiable, according to the subcommentary of Vairocanarakṣita (Kano 2008: 353), phrase I (H) should read *nārthaḥ kaścid asti*. I therefore print this in the Sanskrit text.

Since both of these reconstructions are, with the exception noted above and that discussed below under (B), nothing but speculation, I translate the Tibetan text, distinguishing this translation from that of the extant Sanskrit by use of a smaller type size.

Lévi's proposal, which has been adopted (uncritically, it seems to me) by almost all scholars, runs as follows, with the insertion of the first verse from his verse manuscript (in roman typeface):

I

A) *mahāyāne traidhātukaṁ vijñaptimātraṁ vyavasthāpyate* | B) *cittamātram bho jinaputrā yad uta traidhātukam iti sūtrāt* | C) *cittaṁ mano vijñānaṁ vijñaptiś ceti paryāyāḥ* | D) *cittam atra sasaṁprayogam abhipretaṁ* | E) *mātram ity arthapratiṣedhārthaṁ* |

> vijñaptimātram evaitad asadarthāvabhāsanāt |
> yathā taimirikasyāsatkeśacandrādidarśanam ||

II

A) *atra codyate* |

> *yadi vijñaptir anarthā niyamo na deśakālayoḥ* |
> *santānānasyāniyamaś ca yuktā kṛtyakriyā yuktā na ca* || 2 ||

B) *kim uktaṁ bhavati* | C) *yadi vinā rūpādyarthena rūpādivijñaptir utpadyate na rūpādyarthāt* | D) *kasmāt kvaciddeśa utpadyate na sarvatra* | E) *tatraiva ca deśe kadācid utpadyate na sarvadā* | F) *taddeśakālapratiṣṭhitānāṁ sarveṣāṁ saṁtāna utpadyate na kevalam ekasya* | G) *yathā taimirikāṇāṁ saṁtāne keśādyābhāso nānyeṣāṁ* | H) *kasmād yat taimirikaiḥ keśabhramarādi dṛśyate tena keśādikriyā na kriyate na ca tadanyair na kriyate* | I) *yad annapānavastraviṣāyudhādi svapne dṛśyate tenānnādikriyā na kriyate na ca tadanyair na kriyate gandharvanagareṇāsattvān nagarakriyā na kriyate na ca tadanyair na kriyate* | J) *tasmād arthābhāve deśakāla-*

Nasu Jisshū (1953: 114) suggested some modifications on this reconstruction, with somewhat more attention to the Tibetan translation:

I

A) *mahāyāne traidhātukaṁ vijñaptimātraṁ vyavasthāpyate* | B) *cittamātram idaṁ bho jinaputrā yad uta traidhātukam iti sūtre vacanāt* | C) *cittaṁ mano vijñānaṁ vijñaptir iti paryāyāḥ* | D) *tac ca cittam iha sasaṁprayogam abhiprāyaḥ* | E) *mātragrahaṇam arthapratiṣedhārthaṁ* | F) *vijñānam evedam arthapratibhāsam utpadyate* | G) *yathā taimirikānām asatkeśacandrādidarśanam* | H) *na tu kaścid artho 'sti* |

II

A) *atraitac codyate* |

> na deśakālaniyamaḥ santānāniyamo na ca |
> na ca kṛtyakriyā yuktā vijñaptir yadi nārthataḥ || 2 ||

B) *kim uktaṁ bhavati* | C) *yadi vinā rūpādyarthena rūpādivijñaptir utpadyate na rūpādyarthāt* | D) *kasmāt kva cid eva deśa utpadyate na sarvatra* | E) *tatraiva ca deśe kadācid utpadyate na sarvadā* | F) *tatra deśakāle pratiṣṭhitānāṁ sarveṣāṁ saṁtānaniyama utpadyate na kasya cid eva* | G) *yathā taimirikasyaiva saṁtānasya keśādayaḥ dṛśyante nānyeṣāṁ* | H) *kasmād yaḥ taimirikayair dṛśyate keśabhrāmarādiko na keśādikriyāṁ karoti tadanye tu kurvanti* | I) *svapne paśyamāno 'nnapāna-vastraviṣāyudhādiko nānnapānādikriyāṁ karoti tadanye tu kurvanti abhūtagandharvanagaraṁ na nagarakriyāṁ karoti tadanye tu kurvanti* | J) *vinārthena eṣv asatsamaneṣu deśakāla-*

A)
There is little question that the first word of the treatise is indeed *Mahāyāne*. For this reason I translate as I do, a bit unnaturally in English. Better would be "according to the Great Vehicle," but in order to preserve the priority of the fundamental term *mahāyāna*, I make this choice in English.
B)
This scripture citation has been much discussed. As La Vallée Poussin (1912: 67n3) and Lévi (1932: 43n1) point out, it should undoubtedly be traced to the *Daśabhūmika-sūtra* (Kondō 1936: 98.8–9), which contains the sentence *cittamātram idaṁ yad idaṁ traidhātukam*. Various forms of the same are found cited in a range of sources. The inclusion of *bho jinaputrā*, and whether, with Tibetan *dag*, it should be taken as a plural, seems to me to have unnecessarily occupied the attentions of Harada 2000 who, however, does not pay attention to some of the citations offered by Lévi in the above mentioned note (he confessed in 1999: 101n2 that he did not "yet" have access to this book). See also for useful references Harada 2003.
C)
Lévi (1932: 43n2) points to *Abhidharmakośa* II 34ab (Pradhan 1975: 22) *cittaṁ mano 'tha vijñānam ekārthaṁ*, which of course does not take account of *vijñapti*.
FG)
While the Tibetan (and Chinese) translations present these two sentences as prose, the separate Sanskrit manuscript of the verses of the *Viṁśatikā* preserves instead a verse:

> vijñaptimātram evedam asadarthāvabhāsanāt |
> yadvat taimirakasyāsatkeśoṇḍūkādidarśanam ||

> This [world] is just Manifestation-Only, because of the appearance of non-existent external objects, as in the case of the seeing of nonexistent hair-nets and so on by one with an eye disease.

There is some discussion concerning the reading of the word *keśoṇḍūka*. In particular, how to read the shape under *ṇḍ* has been questioned. Dictionaries tell us to expect *-u-*, but a reading with the manuscript of *ū* is superior from a metrical point of view. On the first two verses see Funahashi 1986 (perhaps one of the first, if not the very first, to have made direct use of the Nepalese manuscripts); not much seems to have been added by Hanneder 2007.

As already noted by La Vallée Poussin (1912: 67n7, and see Lévi 1932: 44n1), the same verse is quoted in the *Lokatattvanirṇaya* of the Jaina scholar Haribhadrasūri, where it appears in the following form (verse I.74; Suali 1905: 283.16–284.1): *vijñaptimātram evaitad asamarthāvabhāsanāt | yathā taimirakasyeha kośakīṭādidarśanam ||*, in which at the very least *kośa°* must be read *keśa°*. [Ui 1917:2–3 cites the verse, crediting La Vallée Poussin for its discovery and identification, although most Japanese scholars appear to overlook the clear attribution offered by Ui, as well as La Vallée Poussin's earlier article itself.]

For a partial translation and some observations on Dharmapāla's commentary on *timira*, see Chu 2004: 120ff.

III

As La Vallée Poussin (1912: 70n1, followed by Lévi 1932: 46n1) points out, we find a parallel in the *Nyāyavārttika* (he refers to 528.12 in an edition not available to me; in the edition of Tarkatirtha 1944: 1085.9–13): *asaty arthe vijñānabhedo dṛṣṭa iti cet | atha manyase yathā tulyakarmavipākotpannāḥ pretāḥ pūyapūrṇāṁ nadīṁ paśyanti | na tatra nady asti na pūyam | na hy ekaṁ vastv anekākāraṁ bhavitum arhati | dṛṣṭaś ca vaijñānabhedaḥ | kecit tām eva jalapūrṇaṁ paśyanti kecid rudhirapūrṇāṁ ity ato 'vasīyate yathā 'dhyātme nimittāpekṣam asati bāhye nimitte vijñānam eva tathotpadhyate iti.* This is translated by Jha (1919: 261) as follows: "'But even in the absence of real objects we find diversity in the cognitions.' You mean by this as follows: —'From among persons born under the influence of similar destinies, while some (on death) have sight of a river full of pus—though in reality neither the river nor the pus are there; and though one and the same thing cannot have several forms, yet in regard to the same *river* we find diversity in the cognitions: Some other persons see that same river as full of water, others again as full of blood, and so forth; from all [of] which it follows that in each case the Cognition appears in that particular form in accordance with the inner consciousness of each person, and it has no external basis in the shape of an object.'" The passage continues (Tarkatirtha 1944: 1085.16–1086.4; Jha 1919: 262): *deśādiniyamaś ca prāpnoti* | *ekasmin deśe nadīṁ pūyapūrṇāṁ paśyanti no deśāntareṣu* | *asaty arthe niyamahetur vaktavyaḥ* | *yasya punar vidyamānaṁ kenacid ākāreṇa vyavasthitaṁ tasya śeṣo mithyāpratyaya iti yuktam* | *mithyāpratyayāś ca bhavanto na pradhānaṁ bādhanta iti pūyādipratyayānāṁ pradhānaṁ vaktavyam iti* | *yathā pūyādipratyayānām evaṁ māyāgandharvanagaramr̥gatr̥ṣṇāsalilānām iti* |. "Further (under the Opponent's doctrine) there can be no restriction as to place &c.; that is, when no object exists, what would be the reason for the fact that persons see the river of pus in one place, and not another? He for whom there is something really existing in a definite form,—for him it is quite possible that all cognition in any other form should be wrong; and wrong cognitions, if they appear, never completely discard (do away with) their (real) counterpart; so that it behoves the Opponent to explain what is the counterpart of the cognitions of 'pus' and the rest; and just as in the case of the cognition of 'pus' so also in the case of the cognitions of magical phenomena, imaginary cities, miragic water and so forth (it would be necessary to point to real counterparts)."

CD)

Tib. takes *katham* as a separate question, thus for the sake of indicating the correspondence between the versions I add (D) to the Sanskrit text, although in fact there is no boundary here.

DE)

Note that *vināpy arthena* is translated both *don med par* and *don med par yang* in (D) and (E) respectfully. Moreover, the same phrase is translated with the latter in XVI (C), and with the former in XVII (E).

E)

Tib. has no equivalent for *kāla*, instead reading *yul la sogs pa*, 'place etc'.

I)

Tib. has no equivalent for *samaṁ*, which I also do not see in Vinītadeva (176b6–7).

M)

For the Skt. text's *mūtrapurīṣādi*, Tib. has *gcin dang | ngan skyugs dang | me ma mur dang | mchil ma dang | snabs*, namely *mūtrapurīṣa*, with the addition of hot ashes (**kukkula*), phlegm/saliva (**kheṭa*), and snot/mucus (**siṅghāṇaka*). The last two are a set combination, as are the first two, but the inclusion of ashes I have not noticed elsewhere in such a context. The commentary of Vinītadeva and the translations of Paramārtha and Xuanzang agree almost completely with the Skt. text, but Prajñāruci (T. 1588 [XXXI] 65b8–9) lists pus 膿, blood 血, urine 小便, feces 大便, liquid iron 流鐵, and flowing water 流水.

IV

I)

In brackets "see" is added on the basis of Tibetan *mthong*.

J)

Chu (2011: 36): "The word *ādhipatya* is a special term in the Yocācāra system: it refers to the mutual influence between different living beings."

L)

Tib. reverses the order of "dogs and crows" (and adds "et cetera") both with respect to the Skt. and its own mention in (H) above.

V

A)

Tib. has *kyang* (**api*) after its equivalent of *tiraścāṁ*.

B)

Tib. has *yang* (**api*) after its equivalent of *narakeṣu*.

F)

Tib. *yi dags kyi bye brag dag* suggests **pretaviśeṣāṇām* in place of the text's *pretāṇām*.

VI

B)

The *Abhidharmakośabhāṣya* (Pradhan 1975: 164.2–4) speaks of: "The forest of iron thorn trees, the sharp thorns of which are 16 fingers long. The thorns turn themselves downwards on beings who climb them, tearing their bodies, and turn themselves upwards on those who descend," *ayaḥśālmalīvanaṁ tīkṣṇaṣoḍaśāṅgulakaṇṭakam | teṣāṁ sattvānām abhirohatāṁ kaṇṭakā avāṅmukhībhavantaḥ kāyaṁ bhindanti avataratāṁ cordhvībhavantaḥ*.

6c

On the function of *go* in the Tib. see Silk 2016. I do not understand the reading in the *Vṛtti* with *'dug* in place of *'dod*, found in the verse-only translation.

D)

Two cases of *der* (**tatra*) in the Tib. trans. do not have any correspondent in Skt.

VII

7ab: La Vallée Poussin (1912: 73n4) points out that the half-verse is found in the *Nyāyavārttika* 529.7 (in the edition of Tarkatirtha 1944: 1086.4; Jha 1919: 262).

D)

Tib. *smras pa* often renders *āha* (as it does in XIV [I], below)

VIII

B)

An important passage for trying to understand the text here is no doubt that in the *Abhidharmakośabhāṣya* chapter 9 (Pradhan 1975: 468.10–15; Lee 2005: 90.1–8; cf. La Vallée Poussin 1923–1931, v.258): *asty eva pudgalo yasmād uktaṁ* nāsti sattva upapāduka *iti mithyādr̥ṣṭiḥ* | *kaś caivam āha* nāsti sattva upapāduka *iti* | *sattvas tu tathāsti yathā vibhakto bhagavateti brūmaḥ** | *tasmād yaḥ paratropapādukasattvākhyaskandhasaṁtānāpavādaṁ karoti tasyaiṣā mithyādr̥ṣṭir* nāsti sattva upapāduka *iti* | *skandhānām upapādukatvāt* | *athaiṣā mithyādr̥ṣṭiḥ pudgalāpavādikā satī kiṁprahātavyā bhavet* | *na hy eṣā satyadarśanabhāvanāprahātavyā yujyate* | *pudgalasya satyeṣv anantarbhāvāt* |. A very tentative translation of this passage might run: "[The Pudgalavādins assert that] the person really exists because the expression "There does not exist a spontaneously born being" was called a mistaken view. But who [claimed] in this way that "There does not exist a spontaneously born being"? We rather assert that a being does exist, [however] in just the fashion analyzed by the Blessed One. Therefore, this mistaken view that "There does not exist a spontaneously born being" belongs to whomever denies that a continuum of aggregates denominated 'being' may be spontaneously born in another [realm], because it is a fact that the aggregates are spontaneously born. Now, if [you hold that] this denial of the person is a mistaken view, [you must state] how it could be abandoned. For it is not reasonable that it could be abandoned by [the four noble] truths, by vision or by mental cultivation, because the person is not included in the [four noble] truths." *: The MS adds *mānuṣyakasūtre*, but this seems to be an error. See Lee 2005: 90n340, Honjō 2014: 905, §9024. The expression *na 'tthi sattā opapātikā* does occur, however, in MN (117) iii.71,30, *Mahācattārīsakasutta*. More investigation is required to understand the relation between Vasubandhu's positions in the present passage and in the *Abhidharmakośabhāṣya*. Note also that the statement denying the existence of the spontaneously arisen being (*nāsti sattva upapādukaḥ*) is found cited in several sources, such as the *Saṁghabhedavastu* of the Mūlasarvāstivāda Vinaya (Gnoli 1978: 220.28), and the *Prasannapadā* (La Vallée Poussin 1903–1913: 356.7, at which point La Vallée Poussin's n6 refers to DN i.55,18, which contains the same sequence). See also the following.

C)

This half verse is frequently cited, for instance in the *Abhidharmakośabhāṣya* chapter 9 (Pradhan 1975: 466.9; Lee 2005: 74.12), *Prasannapadā* (La Vallée Poussin 1903–1913: 355.4) and in the *Paramārthagāthā* 4cd (Wayman 1961: 168).

IX

F)

Should we follow the expression in (D) and restore tasyāḥ ⟨*vijñaptes*⟩? Note that Tib. has the term neither in (F) nor above in (D).

G)

The expression ity aya[m] (*abhi*)**prāyaḥ** is rendered in Tib. *'di ni 'dir dgongs pa'o*, which might suggest that we restore instead (*atrābhi*)-prāyaḥ, but there does not appear to be enough room in the missing portion of the manuscript leaf to allow this.

X

A)

The expression *ko guṇaḥ* appears to be idiomatic. Edgerton (1953 s.v. guṇa) suggests that the meaning 'advantage,' for which he refers to the *Mahāvastu*, "is not recorded in this use" in Skt. or Pāli. For another example in a work of Vasubandhu, see the *Abhidharmakośabhāṣya* (Pradhan 1975: 439,6). I have the impression that it occurs in non-Buddhist works as well.

C)

The reconstruction of Tibetan *drug po gnyis* presents problems. What is visible in the MS is *dva*, and *va* is certain. We must reconstruct *vijñāna*, of course. The expression in question means 'two sets of six' or 'two times six,' namely twelve, the twelve āyatanas (Vinītadeva 183a6–183b1). The, or a, normal Sanskrit way to say this, however, is *dviṣaṣ*, but there is no vowel above *dva*. Paramārtha has here (T. 1589 [XXXI] 71c29) 從唯六雙但六識生, and Xuanzang (T. 1590 [XXXI] 75b28) 謂若了知從六二法有六識轉. I follow the suggestion of Harunaga Isaacson that we reconstruct dva(*ya*)ṣ[a](*ṭkābhyāṁ vijñā*)**na**ṣaṭkaṁ, without—as Isaacson emphasizes—insisting that this was indeed the original reading. But it certainly fits the context.

For the Skt. *mantā*, Tib. has *reg pa po* = **spraṣṭā*. Paramārtha has this same reading (見者乃至爲觸者), as does Vinītadeva (183b1), while Xuanzang has 見者乃至知者 and Prajñāruci (T. 1588 [XXX] 67a1) 覺者, agreeing with *mantā*. Akashi (1926: 160n2) wonders whether we should emend the Tibetan to *rig pa po* (which Sasaki 1924: 48 prints), but seems unconvinced by his own suggestion. *reg pa po* corresponds to the fifth, but not the sixth, item in the relevant list. The confusion, wherever it lies, seems to come from the (apparent?) contradiction of the presentation in IX (C-E), which limits itself to the visible through the tangible, but X (C) then states the listing to contain 2 × 6 = 12 members, not 10. One version of a listing is found in the *Mañjuśrīvikrīḍitā*: *mthong pa po, nyan pa po, snom pa po, za ba po, reg pa po, rnam par shes pa po* = *draṣṭā, śrotā, ghrātā, bhoktā, spraṣṭā, vijñātā* (draft ed. J. Braarvig at https://www2.hf.uio.no). The (non-Buddhist) list in the *Mahābhārata* is slightly different (14.20.21): *ghrātā bhakṣayitā draṣṭā spraṣṭā śrotā ca pañcamaḥ* | *mantā boddhā ca saptaite bhavanti paramartvijaḥ* ||. The matter should be carefully considered, paying attention also to Vinītadeva's commentary.

10c

The Tibetan translation of the verses has *bstan pas* for what in the *Vṛtti* is read *bstan pa'i* (D: *bstan pa*).

H)

Tib. adds *yang* after its equivalent of *vijñaptimātram iti*, with *rnam par rig pa tsam zhes bya ba de yang med pas* representing something like **vijñaptimātram ity tad api nāst(īt)i*, instead of *tad api vijñaptimātraṁ* *nāstīti*, although it seems that *iti* is made to do double duty here as the quotative *zhes bya ba* and as the reason represented by *pas*.

J)

api tu is not represented in Tib.

K)

Skt. *grāhyagrāhakādiḥ parikalpitas* is omitted in Tib.

L)

Tib. has its equivalent for *na tv anabhilāpyenātmanā yo buddhānām viṣaya iti* as *sangs rgyas kyi yul gang yin pa brjod du med pa'i bdag nyid kyis ni med pa ma yin no*, which La Vallée Poussin (1912: 76) rendered: "mais elles [= les choses, *dharmāḥ*] ne sont pas sans exister de l'indicible manière d'être qui est du domaine des Bouddhas." Paramārtha has (T. 1589 [XXXI] 72a9–10) 不由不可言體諸佛境界說諸法空, and Xuanzang (T. 1590 [XXXI] 75c8) 非諸佛境離言法性亦都無故名法無我, the latter of which suggests something closer, perhaps, to the Tib. understanding.

M)

For *nairātmyapraveśo* Tib. has *chos la bdag med par 'jug pa*, **dharmanairātmyapraveśo*, as we see in (I).

XII

12:

La Vallée Poussin (1912: 78n1, with additions by Lévi 1932: 52n1) notes a number of citations of this verse, including Prajñākaramati's *Bodhicaryāvatārapañjikā ad* IX.87 (La Vallée Poussin 1901–1914: 503.7, with the expression *yad uktam ācāryapādaiḥ*) and *Nyāyavarttika* (Tarkatirtha 1944: 1068.20–21; Jha 1919: 243), and see La Vallée Poussin's detailed note to his translation of the *Sarvadarśanasaṁgraha* (1901–1902: 179n77), as well as the citation in the *Sarvasiddhāntasaṁgraha* III.12 (edited in La Vallée Poussin 1901–1902: 403).

12b

Here and below, Tib. renders Skt. *mātra* with *tsam* but (as here) when it means 'extent' not 'only,' perhaps Tib. *tshod* would be better.

G)

In the manuscript we find the reading *niravayatvāt*, for what we would expect as *niravayavatvāt*, and the same in XIII (B). The form *niravayava* is well attested, for instance in *Brahmasūtra* 2.1.26: *kr̥tsnaprasaktir niravayavatvaśabdakopo vā.* However, there are also a number of instances in which the form without final *-va* also appears. It is not possible at this moment to be absolutely sure that they are erroneous. In the *Ekādaśamukhahr̥dayam* (Dutt 1939: 35–40; input and corrected by Somadeva Vasudeva at http://gretil.sub.uni-goettingen.de/gretil/1_sanskr/4_rellit/buddh/ekmuhr_u.htm, based on the published manuscript [see von Hinüber 2014: 104, item 33a]), corresponding to Dutt's 38.5–8 we find *evaṁ mahārthiko 'yaṁ mama bhagavat hr̥*[*dayam*] *ekavelāṁ prakāśitvā catvāro mūlāpattayaḥ kṣa*[*yaṁ*] *gacchanti* | *pañcānantaryāṇi karmāṇi niravaya<va>ṁ tanvīkariṣya<n>ti* | *kaḥ punar vādo athābhāṣitaṁ pratipatsyanti* |. Here Vasudeva has restored the form *niravayava*, although the manuscript writes only *niravaya.* In the edition of the *Mīmāṁsāślokavārttika* with the commentary *Kāśikā* of Sucaritamiśra we find (sub 5.4.103) a sentence printed *yadā kaścit sautrāntikaṃ pratyevaṃ sādhayati* | *ātmā nityaḥ niravayatvāt vyomavad iti tadā dharmadharmidvayasya bādhanaṃ bhavati.* However, Kei Kataoka writes to me as follows (email 11 IX 2014): "I checked the Adyar manuscript of the *Kāśikā*. It has *anavayavatvāt* on p. 1863.6. (neither *niravayavatvāt* nor *niravayatvāt*) [manuscript preserved in the Adyar Library, Chennai, No. 63358, TR 66–4]. I noticed another instance of *niravayatve* in the *Nyāyamañjarī*, Mysore edition Vol. II 420.6. But the manuscript reads *niravayavatve* [manuscript preserved in Government Oriental Manuscript Library, Madras (Chennai), R 3583. Malayalam]. So the mistake *niravayavatva* > *niravayatva* does happen." Somdev Vasudeva points out to me several other instances in which at least the electronically available versions of the *Nyāyamañjarī*, Jayatīrtha's *Nyāyasudha* and several other texts also have the latter form, without *-va-*.

I)

Skt. *arthāntaram* is pluralized in Tib. *don gzhan rnams*. There are several other places in this text where the Tibetan appears to be plural corresponding to singular forms in Sanskrit. In this sentence, I follow the advice of Prof. Schmithausen and connect it with the following verse, but note that this is not the understanding of the Tib. translation, or of Frauwallner, who understands things quite a bit differently here (for convenience I cite the English [2010: 402], but the German is the same [1994: 375]): "(Opponent:) The Individual atoms do not combine with one another because they are partless. Thus, this mistake need not result. When aggregated, they do, however, combine with one another; so say the Vaibhāṣikas of Kaśmir. (Answer:) But the amassment of atoms is nothing other than they themselves." The Chinese of Parmārtha renders the passage (T. 1589 [XXXI] 72b3–7): 若汝言:「隣虛不得聚集, 無方分故。此過失不得故起。是隣虛聚更互相應」。罽賓國毘婆沙師作如此說。則應問之: 如汝所説:「隣虛聚物, 此聚不異隣虛」, while Xuanzang has (T. 1590 [XXXI] 76a3–5): 加濕彌羅國毘婆沙師言: 非諸極微有相合義, 無方分故。離如前失。但諸聚色有相合理有方分故。此亦不然. All of these versions, it seems to me, understand the thought to be completed here, rather than continuing into the following verse. Despite this, it is very clear that the Skt. expects a question (*te idaṁ praṣṭavyāḥ*), and the question does not come until 13ab.

XIV

14ab:

La Vallée Poussin (1912: 79n1) notes the citation in Prajñākaramati's *Bodhicaryāvatārapañjikā ad* IX.87 (La Vallée Poussin 1901–1914: 50210–11), and in *Nyāyavārttika* 522.10 (Tarkatirtha 1944: 1070.4; Jha 1919: 245), where it is read as *digdeśabhedo yasyāsti tasyaikatvaṁ na yujyate*.

B)

The MS has *pā* and another illegible character. Tib. *ngos* suggests the restitution pā(*rśv*)e (see already La Vallée Poussin 1912: 80). A problem is that we need *$chāyā$ (Tib. *grib ma 'bab par*), while the text has only *ātapa* ('sunshine'). Moreover, the syntax with *anyatra pārśve bhavaty anyatrātapaḥ* suggests, if it does not make quite certain, that something has dropped out between *pārśve* and *bhavaty*, which I here conjecturally restore as *chāyā*. Under this understanding, Skt. *anyatrātapaḥ* is missing from Tib. However, we find in Vinītadeva (187a7) the following: *gal te rdul phra rab cha shas med pa'i phyir phyogs kyi cha tha dad pa med na de'i dus na nyi ma shar ba'i tshe ngos gcig la grib ma 'bab pa gcig tu nyi ma shar bar ji ltar 'gyur*, indicating that the text available to Vinītadeva must have had something very close to what I conjecture. See Yamaguchi's note in Sasaki 1924: 17 (n3 to §14). We find the following in the *Nyāyavarttika* (Tarkatirtha 1944: 1071.5–10; Jha 1919: 245–246): *chāyāvṛtī tarhi na prāpnutaḥ paramāṇor adeśatvād iti | na deśavattvāc chāyāvṛtī | kiṁ tarhi | mūrtimatsparśavattvāt mūrtimat sparśaviśiṣṭaṁ dravyaṁ dravyāntaram āvṛṇoti | kim idam āvṛṇoti | svasambandhitvenetarasya sambandhaṁ pratiṣedhatīti | chāyā tu tejaḥparamāṇor āvṛṇāt mūrtimatā paramāṇunā tejaḥparamāṇur āvrīyate yan na chāyeti viralatejaḥsambandhīti dravyaguṇakarmāṇi chāyety abhidhīyate sarvato vyāvṛttatejaḥsambandhīni tu tāni tamaḥsaṁjñakānīti | tad evaṁ chāyāvṛtyor anyathāsiddhatvād ahetuḥ |*. "'In that case, as there would be no points of space in the Atom, there should be no shadow, nor screening.' But shadow and screeing are due, not to presence of space-points, but to corporeality and tangibility; it is only a corporeal and tangible object that screens another object. 'What is the meaning of this *screening*?' What it means is that the Object being itself connected (with something) prevents the connection (with that same thing) of another object. *Shadow* also is due to the screening of the atoms of light; i.e., the corporeal Atom screens the atom of Light; and there is 'Shadow' where this screening takes place. In fact 'Shadow' is the name applied to such substances, qualities and actions as are connected with the smaller amount of Light (than the adjacent things); and when those same substances have all light completely turned away from them, they come to be called 'Darkness.' Thus, as the phenomena of 'shadow' and 'screening' are capable of being otherwise explained, they cannot serve as valid reasons (in support of the proposition that Atoms are made up of parts)."

F)

The MS reads sarvaṁ saṁhātaḥ, which I emend to sarvaḥ saṁghātaḥ. Tib. *'dus pa thams cad*. The whole sentence is found as follows in Paramārtha (T. 1589 [XXXI] 72b24–25): 若無有障, 一切六方隣虛同一處故, 則一切聚同隣虛量. These translations demonstrate that *sarva* must govern *saṁghāta*. Note, however, that in Xuanzang (T. 1590 [XXXI] 76a21–23): 既不相礙, 應諸極微展轉處同, 則諸色聚同一極微量, this relation is not made clear (as usual, Prajñāruci will require some sorting out).

I)

The reading of all Tanjurs, *yin no*, must be emended in light of the Skt. to **ma yin no*. Vinītadeva's commentary (187b6) has *mdo sde pas smras pa ma yin no zhes bya ba smos so*. See Yamaguchi's note in Sasaki 1924: 17 (n5 to §14).

14cd

vānyo na] MS (B): vā anyonya; MS (A): vā syātāṁ na. Part of the confusion of the reading may have come about by the commentary's dissolution of the feet of the verse. Tib. has lines cd as *grib dang sgrib par ji ltar 'gyur gong bu gzhan min de de'i min*, (PT 125: *drib dang sgrib kyang ji ltar 'gyur phung myin gal te de de myin*). For cd Paramārtha has (T. 1589 [XXXI] 74b1): 影障復云何 若同則無二, while Xuanzang has (T. 1590 [XXXI] 76a16): 無應影障無 聚不異無二. These versions variously suggest the presence in cd of *anya—gzhan, kyang*, 同 = *anya na*, more literally 不異. At the same time, however, the *'gyur* might suggest itself as an equivalent for *syātāṁ*, although in the prose of (H) where precisely this verb is found in Skt. it is translated with *yin*.

M)

Tib. appears to have taken this as a verse. However, none of the Chinese versions do so, and the Skt. as we have it is not metrical.

Lévi (1932: 54n1) quotes (and translates) the *Sphuṭārthā Abhidharmakośavyākhyā* of Yaśomitra (Wogihara 1936: 26.11–16) as follows: *Vaibhāṣikāṇām ayam abhiprāyaḥ. nīlādigrahaṇam ātapālokagrahaṇaṁ vā saṁsthānanirapekṣaṁ pravartate. kāyavijñaptigrahaṇaṁ tu varṇanirapekṣaṁ. pariśiṣṭarūpāyatanagrahaṇaṁ tu varṇasaṁsthānāpekṣaṁ pravartata iti. Sautrāntikapākṣikas tu ayam ācāryo nainam arthaṁ prayacchati. na hi cākṣuṣam etat saṁsthānagrahaṇaṁ. mānasaṁ tv etat parikalpitaṁ.*

XV

B)

The emendation to *nyes pa* is supported by the sense, the Skt. and Vinītadeva (188a7): *gcig bu'i nyes pa 'ang bshad pa nyid de.* See also Yamaguchi's note in Sasaki 1924: 18 (n8 to §14).

C)

Tib. *sngon po dang ser po la sogs pa gang yin pa* suggests **nīlapītādika.* Schmithausen suggests the reading and restoration *n(īlādi)kañ*, writing that the "akṣara nā in the ms. may well be a mutilated nī." This is certainly an attractive solution; immediately earlier in the line in the word sūkṣmānīkṣā (MS: śūkṣmānīkṣā) we see the akṣara nī, the shape of which is compatible with what is left here at the end of the line (without color photos it is difficult to tell more), and there is likely enough space for two additional akṣaras, as Schmithausen suggests. The Chinese versions have: Prajñāruci (T. 1588 [XXXI] 68b2–4): 若純一青物不雜黄等, 若人分別眼境界者, 行於地中不得說言有次第行; Paramārtha (T. 1589 [XXXI] 72c8–9): 若一切青黄等無有隔別, 是眼境界執爲一物, 於地則無次第行; Xuanzang (T. 1590 [XXXI] 76b4–5): 若無隔別所有青等, 眼所行境執爲一物, 應無漸次行大地理. Paramārtha's version agrees with Tib. in listing blue and yellow, while the others have only blue, supporting the suggested restoration of Skt.

Skt. *gamanam ity arthaḥ* looks like a gloss to clarify *krameṇetir*; it is omitted in Tib., but it is possible that in Prajñāruci's translation cited immediately above, 不得說言有次第行, "we cannot say that there is gradual motion," is meant to stand for *na syād gamanam ity arthaḥ*. Verhagen (1996: 39n95–40n96) points to similar expressions in the *Abhidharmakośabhāṣya* (Pradhan 1975: 138.2), *eti gaty-arthaḥ*, and in the *Prasannapadā* (La Vallée Poussin 1903–1913: 5.1), *etir gaty-arthaḥ*.

E)

The Skt. MS's *anekatra* (MS *hastyaśvādikasyānekatra*) is understood in Tib. (*gcig na*) and elsewhere as **ekatra*. Vinītadeva (188b7): *de'i tshe gnas gcig gi steng na 'dug pa'i glang po che dang rta la sogs pa du ma ris su chad par 'dug par mi 'gyur ro*; Prajñāruci (T. 1588 [XXXI] 68b13) 一處, and Xuanzang (T. 1590 [XXX] 76b7) 一方處 (Paramārtha [T. 1589 (XXXI) 72c11] is unclear). There is no easily imaginable graphic way to account for the manuscript reading as a writing error.

F)

I restore the lacuna in the MS vicche(*do yujya*)**te** in light of Tib. *rung*. That is, *de dag ris su chad par ji ltar rung* = kathaṁ tayor vicche(*do yujya*)**te**.

G)

The MS has *tadaikaṁ*, for which I read *tad ekam*. However, Tib. *de dag gcig tu* might suggest **te ekaṁ*(?).

I add 'reasonable' on the basis of Tib. *rung*. See (F) above.

H)

On the grammatical function of *go* in the Tib. see Silk 2016.

J)

Tib. *de dag* seems to correspond to Skt. *sa*.

XVI

16c

I do not understand Tib. *khyod kyi don* as equivalent of *so 'artha*.

D)

Tib. *yul 'di nyid* apparently corresponds to *idam*. Here the expression yad(*ā*) ca sā pratyakṣa(*buddhir bhava*)**tī**daṁ me pratyakṣam iti is rendered *gang gi tshe yul 'di nyid ni bdag gi mngon sum mo snyam du mngon sum gyi blo de byung ba*, but above in (B) ity asaty arthe ka(*tham*) iyaṁ buddhir bha(*vatīdaṁ me*) pratyakṣam iti is rendered *don de med na 'di ni bdag gi mngon sum mo snyam pa blo 'di ji ltar 'byung zhe na*.

Skt. *na so ⟨'⟩rtho dṛśyate* appears in Tib. as *khyod kyi don de mi snang ste*.

In *manovijñānenaiva*, Tib. has no equivalent for *eva*.

EF)

The Skt. expressions iti kathaṁ tasya pratyakṣatvam iṣṭaṁ | viśeṣ(*e*)ṇa tu kṣaṇika(++++)**ya**sya tadānīṁ niruddham eva tad rūpaṁ rasādikaṁ vā | correspond to Tib. *lhag par yang skad cig mar smra bas de mngon sum du ji ltar 'dod* || *de ltar na de'i tshe gzugs dang rol sogs pa de dag ni 'gags zin to* || This suggests something like **kathaṁ kṣāṇikavādinā tasya pratyakṣatvam iṣṭam | evaṁ tu tadānīṁ niruddhaṁ tadrūpaṁ rasādikaṁ vā,* perhaps: 'How do the advocates of the doctrine of momentariness accept direct perception of that [object], given that at that time visible form, flavor and the rest have entirely ceased in that fashion?' Lévi suggested restoring (*sya viṣa*), but I see no trace of **viṣaya* in Tib. I follow Schmithausen (following Tib. and Frauwallner) in offering kṣaṇika(*vādino*). Paramārtha (T. 1589 [XXXI] 73a2–4) has: 是塵云何可證, 若人說剎那滅。此人是時執色乃至觸已謝, while Xuanzang translates (T. 1590 [XXXI] 76b24–25): 剎那論者有此覺時, 色等現境亦皆已滅。如何此時許有現量. While the first two support the restitution of *vādin*, Xuanzang's version seems close to that in Tib.

XVII

H)

Tib. *yod pa ma yin pa* as a translation of *abhūta*, which below is *yang dag pa ma yin pa*.

L)

Tib. *gtan tshigs*, here equivalent to *jñāpaka*, elsewhere renders *kāraṇa*. I wonder if this could be due to a confusion, in light of, for example, *Mahāvyutpatti* §4460 *jñapakahetu = shes par byed pa'i gtan tshigs*.

M)

The *Nyāyabhāṣya* (Tarkatirtha 1944: 1077.4–1078.5; Jha 1919: 255) argues as follows: *svapnānte cāsanto viṣayā upalabhyante ity atrāpi hetvabhāvaḥ | pratibodhe 'nupalambhād iti cet | pratibodhaviṣayopalambhād apratiṣedhaḥ | yadi pratibodhe 'nupalambhāt svapne viṣayā na santīti tarhi ya ime pratibuddhena viṣayā upalabhyante upalambhāt santīti | viparyaye hi hetusāmarthyam | upalambhāt sadbhāve saty anupalambhād abhāvaḥ siddhyati ubhayathā tv abhāve nānupalambhasya sāmarthyam asti.* "In fact there is no reason to show that what are cognised during dreams are non-existent things. 'Inasmuch as things dreamt of are not perceived when the man wakes up, (they must be regarded as *non-existent*).' [According to this reasoning of yours] inasmuch as we do apprehend the things cognised during the waking state, the existence of these cannot be denied; if, from the fact of our not apprehending, on waking, the things cognised in dreams, you infer that these things are not existent,—then it follows that the things that we do apprehend when awake are *existent*, because they *are* apprehended; so that the reason you put forward (in proof of the unreality of things dreamt of) is found to have the power of proving a conclusion contrary to your tenets. It is only when the existence of things can be inferred from their apprehension, that you can infer their non-existence from their non-apprehension. And if under both circumstances (of dream as well as of waking) things were equally non-existent, then non-apprehension could have no power at all (of proving anything)."

N)

Tib. *ma sad kyi bar du* for *aprabuddha* understands it as 'while they are not awake.'

XVIII

B)

In *sadasatsaṁparke*, Tib. omits *sadasat*.

18a

On *ādhipatya* see the note above to IV(J).

C)

The expression *yathāyogam*, 'according to the circumstances,' is explained by Vinītadeva (192a3–4) as referring to the ways in which one manifests good and bad physical forms in response to interactions with good and evil companions, and the same with good and bad teachings producing mental forms, although there are no externally existing actions at all.

18cd

Chu (2011: 36) refers to Dharmakīrti's *Santānāntarasiddhi* and its commentary (so far available only in fragments), which a propos *anyādhipatya* (see the verse here, 18a) reads: *vijñānavādino middhābhibhavavibhramād eva puṁso 'nyasya jñānasyādhipatyaṃ sahakāritvaṁ* | *tena śūnyasya jñānasya vṛttir bhaviṣyati* |. "For the Vijñāvādin, precisely for the reason of being overpowered by torpor, of illusion, the influence of another person's cognition is [only] a co-operative causal factor (*sahakāritva*), the cognition empty of that [influence] would take place."

H)

In *arthasadbhāvaḥ*, Tib. omits *sad*.

XIX

A)

Skt. *idam* is rendered *'di dag*, and precisely the same in XXI (A), where again we get the expression *yadi vijñaptimātram evedaṁ* rendered *gal te 'di dag rnam par rig pa tsam*.

Ui (1953: 21 from back) emends the MS's *anukramyamāṇānām* to *upakramyamāṇānām*, and I accept this, although it is hard to explain how the error might have come about. Kano (2008: 356) cites the suggestion of Schmithausen to read *anupakramyamāṇānām* (Prof. Schmithausen suggests to me that this arose through the simple omission of *-pa-* in the MS). A meaning of *upa*$\sqrt{}$*kram*, however, is 'attack, do violence to,' and thus its usage here seems to me fitting. All Chinese versions support this as well. Tib. *gsod pa* is also used by Vinītadeva

(193a1). Prof. Schmithausen, however, writes to me: "Actually, a negation is found here in Paramārtha's rendering of the passage .... In this case, we may translate: "If everywhere there is only vijñapti, then there is no body and no speech. Why should cows, sheep and other animals, without being injured by the butchers, die? If their death is not effectuated by the butchers, why are the butchers guilty of killing living beings?" Paramārtha's version reads (T. 1589 [XXXI] 73b8–10): 問: 若一切唯有識, 則無身及言。云何牛、羊等畜生非屠兒所害而死。若彼死非屠兒所作, 屠兒云何得殺生罪. The passage in Xuanzang's translation reads (T. 1590 [XXXI] 76c27–28): 若唯有識無身語等, 羊等云何爲他所殺。若羊等死不由他害, 屠者云何得殺生罪: "If there is only consciousness, without body or speech, how are rams and the like killed by others? If rams and the like die without being violently treated by others, how does a butcher produce the sin of killing?" Prajñāruci's translation (T. 1588 [XXXI] 69b4–8) has: 問曰: 若彼三界唯是內心, 無有身口外境界者。以何義故。屠獵師等殺害猪羊及牛馬等。若彼非是屠獵師等殺害猪羊牛馬等者, 以何義故。屠獵師等得殺生罪。是故, 應有外色香等身口境界. At the very least the translation of Xuanzang seems to me to support my suggested reading, with the single negation corresponding to *atatkr̥te vā tanmaraṇe*. Schmithausen suggests that the first negation ("without being injured by the butchers") supports the retention of the negation in **an-upakramyamāṇāṁ*.

F)

Skt. *parājayaḥ* omitted in Tib. (noted already by Lévi 1925b: 18).

The story of Vemacitra is discussed in detail by Lévi (1925b: 17–26), translating a Chinese *Saṁyuktāgama* text (T. 99 [1115] [II] 294c19–295b23) alongside the Pāli of SN XI.9ff. [For Sāraṇa, Lévi refers to his own earlier article (1908: 149–152).] For Lévi (1925b: 25), "Il n'est guère douteux que Vasubandhu, en rappelant 'la défaite de Vemacitra due à la malfaisance mentale de moines forestiers,' ait en vue le sūtra du Saṁyukta Āgama."

G)

Skt. *pareṣāṁ* corresponds to Tib. *sems can gzhan gyi*.

I accept the GNP reading *'byung ste* | *des* under the assumption that *des* is meant to render Skt. *yayā*.

The term *sabhāgasantati* refers to the continuity of moments of mentality, one like moment following the next. Cp. for instance the expression from the *Pitṛputrasamāgama* quoted in the *Śikṣāsamuccaya* (Bendall 1897–1902: 253.5): *anantarasabhāgā cittasaṁtati.*

XX

Lévi (1925b: 26–35) discusses the Upāli sūtra in detail, and as he says (1925b: 27) "Par une rencontre singulière, j'ai découvert à la Bibliothèque du Durbar, à Katmandou, un feuillet où se retrouve la citation incorporée par Vasubandhu dans son commentaire." This folio has been edited anew in Chung and Fukita (2011: 329–337), alongside its Chinese parallel.

C-E)

The quotation in Vasubandhu's text —*kaccit te gṛhapate śrutaṁ kena tāni daṇḍakāraṇyāni mātaṅgāraṇyāni kaliṅgāraṇyāni śūnyāni medhyībhūtāni tenoktaṁ śrutaṁ me bho gautama ṛṣīṇāṁ manaḥpradoṣeṇeti*— is parallel to that found in the Upāli-sūtra edited by Chung and Fukita (2011: 335, §17–19): *(k)iñcit t(e) gṛhapate śrutaṁ santi daṇḍakāraṇyāni kaliṅgāraṇyāni mataṅgāraṇyāni śūnyāni medhyāny araṇyabhūtānīti* | *śrutam me bho gautama* | *kiñcit te gṛhapate śrutaṁ kena tāni daṇḍakāraṇyāni kaliṅgāraṇyāni mataṅgāraṇyāni śūnyāni medhyāny araṇyabhūtānīty* | … (§25) *śrutaṁ me bho gautama riṣīṇāṁ manaḥprakopenti.*

XXI

A)

See note to XIX (A) above.

B)

This expression, which is found in Tib. and Xuanzang but not the other two Chinese versions, may be meant to be Vasubandhu's words, but might be a rhetorical device of the opponent.

D)

I take the liberty of quoting in full, with his permission, what Prof. Schmithausen wrote to me:

> D looks defective. We have an objection in the form: If this world is only manifestation, then what about the *paracittavidaḥ*? Do they know others' mind or not (*atha na*)? *kiṁ cātaḥ*? ... What regularly follows in such cases is pointing out difficulties in the case of both alternatives: If (*yadi*) x, then difficulty X; if however (*atha*, very often used in the sense of "if however", "if on the other hand") y, then difficulty Y. What is missing here is Y, which might have run thus: "then how can you maintain that there is only *vijñapti* but no external object [because in this case the object, viz., the mind of others, does exist outside the cognition of the *paracittavid*]" (thus Paramārtha and, similarly, Prajñāruci), or: "then *vijñaptimātratā* would not be proved [in this case]" (Xuanzang). I think there is good reason to assume that a piece of text has dropped out here in part of the manuscript tradition, including ms. B and also the manuscript used by the Tibetan translators.

The Chinese of Paramārtha referred to here reads (T. 1589 [XXXI] 73c2–3): 若不知, 云何得他心通。若知, 云何言識無境. Prajñāruci has (T. 1588 [XXXI] 69c29–70a1): 若不知者, 云何説言知於他心。若實知者, 云何説言無外境界, while Xuanzang (T. 1590 [XXXI] 77a19–21) has: 若不能知, 何謂他心智。若能知者, 唯識應不成。雖知他心, 然不如實. With the exception of what may be a gloss added by Xuanzang (not mentioned by Schmithausen), "although they know other minds, [their knowledge] is not in accord with reality," these three translations agree quite closely with one another.

G)

In accord with the Tib. translation, I attach this to the preceeding. I believe this is also the understanding of Paramārtha (T. 1589 [XXXI] 73c7–8): 此二境界不如是, 此顯現故。能取所取分別未滅故, and Xuanzang (T. 1590 [XXXI] 77a27–28): 此二於境不如實知, 由似外境虛妄顯現故。所取能取分別未斷故.

XXII

D)

Skt. *sarvaprakāraṁ* is omitted in Tib.

Colophon

As noted in the Introduction, the title is given wrongly by the manuscript: for the manuscript reading *Viṁśatikā* we must read, with all other sources, *Viṁśikā* or *Viṁśaka*. It is probably needless to point out that the text contains not twenty verses but either (with MS [A]) twenty two, or (with MS [B]) (most probably) twenty one.

Sanskrit Variant Readings

The two first verses are found only in the independent verse MS (A); the commentary MS (B) is missing the first folio. It begins with *niyamaḥ* on folio 2. Only in the case of verses is an indication of source necessary, since only MS (B) contains the prose commentary.

ac = before correction
pc = after correction.

II
J)
santānāniyamaḥ] MS: wrongly santānānniyamaḥ, as if santānān niyamaḥ.

III
D)
tāvat svapne] MS: tāvan svapne
gramārāmastrīpuruṣādikaṁ] MS: reads bhramarā°. The correction is supported by Tib. and all Chinese versions.
L)
pūyapūrṇṇān] MS: ac pūyaṁ pūrṇṇan

IV
C)
anyānyair] MS: anyānair; reading anyonyair would also be possible, but when this Skt. term appears below in XVIII (C) it is translated in Tib. with the very common *phan tshun*, while here we have *gzhan dang gzhan dag gis*.

V
B)
tiryak°] I read a virāma under the ka.
5b
yathā na] MS (A): erroneously yathā ca
5d
duḥkhan] MS (A): written duṣkhan or duḫkhan
C)
°saṁvarttanīyena] MS: nī added in lower margin in the same script with caret to indicate insertion.

VI

A)

narakapālādisaṁjñāṁ] MS: ac nana° with second na erased.

B)

āgacchanto] MS: āganto

gacchantaḥ] MS: ḥ is not legible or even not present

ayaḥśālmalī°] Parts of two letters visible but undecipherable; malī??

6d

vijñānasya neṣyate] MS (B): vijñāna(sya) neṣ(*ya*)t(*e*)

VII

7c

neṣyate] MS (B): n(e)ṣy(ate), at the very best (mostly illegible)

VIII

8c

uktam] MS (B): ac uktaṁm, possible but not clear.

C)

sahetukāḥ ⟨ || ⟩] MS: sahetukā

IX

9c

dvividhāyatanatvena] MS (A): dvividhāyatatvena

9d

tasyā] MS (A): ac tasyā plus an extra (unnecessary, hence erased) vertical line for long vowel

C)

rūpapratibhāsā] MS (A): ac rūpā°.

utpadyate tac ca] MS: utpadyate | tac ca

E)

pariṇāmaviśeṣaprāptād] MS: pariṇāmaviśeṣād

spraṣṭavya°] MS: spaṣṭavya°

F)

kāyaspraṣṭavyāyatanatvena] MS: kāyaspaṣṭavyāyatatvena

X

C)

dva(*ya*)ṣ[a](*ṭkābhyāṁ vijñā*)**na**ṣaṭkaṁ] MS: dva(+)ṣ.(++ *vijñā*)**na**ṣaṭkaṁ

10b

punar] MS (A): punaḥ

10cd
deśanā dharmmanairātmyapraveśaḥ] MS (B): de[śa]nā dha(r)[m](manai)r-ātmyapraveśaḥ; MS (A): °dharmmyanairātmyapraveśaḥ
10d
kalpitātmanā |] MS (B): ///tātmanā
M)
nairātmyapraveśād] MS: nairātmyapraveśā

XI
11d
paramāṇur na] MS (A): erroneously adds ca in margin by na
D)
vaiśeṣikaiḥ anekaṁ] MS: vaiśeṣikaiḥ | anekaṁ

XII
12a
yugapadyogāt] MS (A): yugpadayogāt
C)
ṣaḍaṅśatā] MS: ṣaḍaṅśatāṁ
D)
parasparāvyatirekād] The MS has a small mark resembling a cursive roman letter v between ra and vya, used to indicate that the vowel is to be extended.
G)
niravayavatvāt] MS (B): niravayatvāt. See in the notes above.
saṁghātās] MS (B): saṁhātās
kāśmīravaibhāṣikāḥ ⟨ | ⟩] MS (B): kāśmīravaibhāṣikās
I)
saṁghāto] MS (B): saṁhāto

XIII
13b
tatsaṁghāte] MS (B): tatsaṁhāte
B)
saṁghātā] MS (B): saṁhātā
niravayavatvāt] MS (B): niravayatvāt (see above XII (G)).
sāvayavasyāpi hi] MS (B): pc sāvayavasyāpi hi with syāpi hi rewritten
saṁghātasya] MS (B): saṁhātasya
13c
na] MS (A): ac nā

13d

tatsaṁyogo na sidhyati] MS (B): ta(tsa)ṁyogo na (s)idhyati; MS (A): ac repeats tatsaṁyogo na sidhyati.

XIV

A)

[p]ū(*rvadig*)[bh](*āgo*)] There seems to have been space for 2 more akṣaras to be restored after *go*.

iti digbhāgabhede] MS (B): iti digbhāga added above line with caret.

14c

chāyāvṛtī] MS (A): °vṛttī

B)

pā(*rśv*)[e] ⟨chāyā⟩ **bha**vaty] MS (B): pā . [e] **bha**vaty, to which I add the conjectured chāyā (see notes above).

F)

sarvaḥ saṁghātaḥ] MS (B): sarvaṁ saṁhātaḥ

14cd

anyo na] MS (B): anyonya; MS (A): syātāṁ na. See the note above.

cen na] MA (A) nna added below line; MS (A): In the margin below tāṁ na pi in another (more modern) hand is written mi li tā. Harunaga Isaacson suggests that this (as militāḥ) may be a gloss on piṇḍa: '[the atoms] connected/combined'.

K)

saṁghāta] MS (B): saṁhāta

XV

15a

krameṇetir] MS (A): krameṇeti

15d

sūkṣmā°] Both MSS: śūkṣmā°

C)

syāt ⟨ | ⟩ gamanam] MS (B): syād gamanam

D)

syāt ⟨ | ⟩ na hi] MS (B): syān na hi

E)

hastyaśvādikasyaikatra] MS (B): hastyaśvādikasyān ekatra. See the discussion above.

na syāt ⟨ | ⟩ F) yatraiva] MS (B): nna syād F) yatraiva

G)

tad ekaṁ] MS (B): tadaikaṁ

I)
avaśyaṁ] MS (B): avavaśyaṁ

XVI
A)
pramāṇānāṁ] MS (B): praṇānāṁ
16a
pratyakṣabuddhiḥ] MS (A): °buddhi
16b
tadā] MS (A): ac tādā

XVII
17b
vijñaptiḥ] MS (A): vijñapti
17d
nāprabuddho] MA (A) nāpraṁbuddho

XVIII
18b
mithaḥ] MS (A): mitha, with tha overwritten.

XIX
A)
upakramya°] MS (B): anukramya° (Ui 1953: 21 from back).
maraṇam] MS (B): ac smaraṇam
B)
tanmaraṇe] MS (B): tat°
19a
maraṇaṁ] MS (A): maraṇa
G)
jīvitendriyavirodhinī] MS (B): jītendriyavirodhinī

XX
20b
ṛṣikopataḥ] MS (B): ṣi of ṛṣi° inserted in top margin
C)
kaccit] MS (B): kacci
F)
karmmaṇā] MS (B): karmmanā

XXI
A)
, atha na] MS (B): atha , na
21b
ayathārthaṁ] MS (A): rtha overwritten, no ṁ visible
21c
ajñānād] MS (A): adds °nā° in top margin with ˇ
G)
°grāhakavikalpasyāpra°] MS (B): pc kalpasyā rewritten in cramped space

XXII
22c
kr̥teyaṁ] MS (A): kr̥tyeyaṁ
22d

Colophon
viṁśatikā] MS (B): ac viṁśitikā
ācāryavasubandhoḥ ||] The scribe adds: grantha<pra>māṇam asya bhāṣyasya 160. MS (A): has the colophon viṁśakāvijñaptiprakaraṇaṁ samāptam ||

Tibetan Variant Readings of the *Vṛtti*

O

bing shi ka bṛtti ||] C: bing shi ka britti ||; D: bingshi ka bṛdhi ||

I

A)
gzhag ste] NP: bzhag ste
B)
mdo las |] CD: mdo las
phyir ro] N: phyiro
C)
rnam par rig pa] N: rnaṁr rig pa
E)
don dgag pa'i phyir ro] P: don dgag gi phyir ro
G)
skra zla] C: ska zla; N: sgra zla

II

2a)
don min na] D: don man na
B)
zhe na |] C: zhe na ||
D)
'byung la] N: 'byung ba
ma yin |] N: ma yin ||
E)
res 'ga'] D: ras 'ga'
'byung la] GN(?)P: 'byung ba
ma yin |] G: ma yin ||
F)
ma yin |] G: ma yin ||
G)
snang gi |] C: snang gi
ma yin ||] P: ma yin |
H)
sbrang bu] D: sgrang bu
byed la |] CG: byed la ||
I)
mi byed la |] CG: mi byed la ||

III

3a
'grub ste ||] C: 'grub sta ||; G: 'grub ste |; NP: 'gyur te |
C)
ji lta] NP: ji ltar
zhe na |] N: zhe na
D)
thams cad na ma yin yul de nyid na yang res 'ga' snang la] GNP: ø
3b
nges pa med |] G: nges pa med ||
3c
yi dags] G: yi dwags (consistently below, not further noted)
G)
rnams kyi dang] N: rnams kyisH)
ji ltar 'grub |] G: ji ltar 'grub ||
J)
rnag gi] N: rnagi
L)
klung rnag gis] GNP: klung rnag gi
M)
rnag gis gang ba] GNP: rnag gi gang ba
me ma mur] GNP: me mar mur
dbyig pa dang |] GP: dbyig pa dang
srung ba] GNP: bsrungs pa

IV

4a
gnod pa 'dra ||] C: gnod pa 'dra |
A)
grub ces] GNP: 'grub ces
rig par bya'o ||] DN rig par bya'o |
C)
bzhi 'grub bo] CDG: bzhin 'grub bo
D)
grub ces] GNP: 'grub ces
E)
pas sems can] N: pas seṁn (occasionally used, without discernable pattern; not noted further)
4c
dmyal ba'i] N: dmyal ba'i |
mthong dang ||] GNP: mthong dang |
G)
sems can rnams kyis] NP: sems can rnams kyi
I)
thams cad kyis mthong gi |] GNP: thams cad kyis mthong gis
gcig 'gas ni] GNP: gcig 'gas na
yin no] N: yino (occassionally below; not further noted)
O)
sems can dmyal ba pa dag go ||] CG: sems can dmyal ba pa dag go |
rnam par gzhag pa] N: rnam par bzhag pa
med par 'gyur ro ||] D: med par 'gyur ro |; N: med par 'gyuro | (such abbreviations not further noted)
P)
gcig gnod pa byed kyang ji lta] C: gcig gnod pa byed kyang ji lta |
ji lta bur] C: ji lta | bur
'jigs par] GNP: 'jig par
Q)
sa gzhi] N: sa bzhi
gnod pa byed par 'gyur |] GNP: gnod pa byed par 'gyur
R)
'byung bar ga la 'gyur |] GN: 'byung bar ga la 'gyur ||

V

A)
'byung ste |] P: 'byung ste || (end of folio)
5c
de ltar] verse version has 'di ltar
E)
de'i phyir] GNP: de'i
yi dags kyi] GNP: yi dags

VI

A)
de dag gi] GNP: de dag gis
las rnams kyis] GNP: las rnams kyi
B)
de lta bur yang 'gyur ste |] CD: de lta bur yang 'grub ste |
dags 'ong ba dang |] N: dags 'ong ba dang ||
shal ma li'i] GNP: shal ma la'i
nags tshal] N: nag tshal
'gyur ba lta bu ste] GNP: 'gyur ba de lta bu ste
6a
de'i las kyis] GNP: de'i las kyi
6b
'byung ba dang] CD: byung ba dang
6c
'dug na go |] D: 'dug na go ||
6d
mi 'dod ||] P: mi 'dod |
D)
mi 'dod la |] CGN: mi 'dod la ||
E)
rnams su rtog |] GNP: rnams su rtog

VII

7b
rtog ||] D: rtog |; GNP: rtogs ||
7d
mi bya ||] N: mi bya |
A)
bag chags de dag] GNP: bag chags dag
B)
rnam par shes par gyur pa] GNP: rnam par shes par 'gyur pa
de 'dra bar] C: de 'da bar
C)
ci yod |] N: ci yod ||
E)
snang gi |] D: snang gi ||
gsung bar mi 'gyur ro] N: gsung par mi 'gyur

VIII

A)
ma yin te |] D: ma yin te ||
8b
'dul ba yi] GNP: 'dul ba'i
8d
rdzus te] CD: brdzus te (P: ba may have been removed)
B)
rdzus te] CD: brdzus te
bzhin yod do ||] GNP: yod do
zhes] C: zhis
sems kyi rgyud] GNP: sems kyi
C)
las byung ||] GN: las byung |

IX

A)
she na |] P: she na ||
9c
de yi] GNP: de'i
B)
zhe na |] N: zhe na ||
C)
de dang | snang ba] CD: de dang snang ba
D)
bcom ldan 'das kyis] GNP: bcom ldan 'das kyi
go rims] G: go rim
E)
bye brag tu] G: bye brag tu pa'i bye brag tu
F)
bcom ldan 'das kyis] G: bcom ldan 'das

X

C)
shes pa drug] P: shes pa
gcig pu] GNP: gcig po
'jug go |] D: 'jug go ||
10c
bstan pa'i] D: bstan pa
10d
'jug 'gyur ||] GNP: 'jug 'gyur |
D)
rig pa tsam du] GNP: rig pa tsam nyid du
F)
nyid gzugs la] N: nyid gzugs (end of line)
G)
mtshan nyid kyi] N: mtshan nyid kyis
'jug go || C: 'jug go |; GNP: 'jug |
L)
sangs rgyas kyi yul] NP: sangs rgyas kyi spyod yul
M)
rtogs pa'i phyir] GNP: rtog pa'i phyir
rnam par gzhag pas] GNP: rnam par bzhag pas
N)
don du 'gyur bas] N: don du 'gyur bas followed by 20 spaces filled with tsegs

XI

A)
dgongs pa 'dis] D: dgongs pa 'das
skye mched yod par] D: skye mched yang par
gzugs la sogs pa] GNP: gzugs la sogs pa'i
rnam par rig pa] N: rnam par rig par
ji ltar rtogs par] GNP: ji ltar rtog par
B)
'di ltar |] CD: 'di ltar
C)
zhe na |] C: zhe na ||
D)
ngo bor brtag pa'i] GNP: ngo bor brtags pa'i
rab du ma 'am] GNP: rab du ma 'am |

XII

A)
ce na |] CD: ce na
'di ltar ||] GNP: 'di ltar
12a
drug gis] GNP: drug gis |
C)
gcig gi go] NP: gcig gis go
12c
gcig na ||] N: gcig na |
D)
ji ste] N: ji snyed
na ni] N: nad (see next)
E)
des na] N: ni na
G)
ma yin gyi |] G: ma yin gyis ||; NP: ma yin gyis |
I)
yin pa de de dag] GNP: yin pa de dag
gzhan rnams] GNP: gzhan nam gzhan

XIII

13d
de] GNP: de'i
B)
rdul phra rab] GNP: rdul phra rab gyi
rnams] N: rnam
shas med] G: shes med
zer cig |] D: zer cig
yang sbyor bar] GNP: yang sbyor bas
C)
de bas] N: de bas na
phra rab rdzas] N: phra rab brdzas
D)
rdul phra rab] C: rdul rab

XIV

A)
rdul phra rab kyi] GP: rdul phra rab gyi
14c
grib dang sgrib] CD: sgrib dang sgrib
B)
re re la phyogs] GNP: re re la yang phyogs
grib ma 'bab par] GNP: grib mi 'bab par
C)
de la ni] N: de lta ni
D)
phyogs kyi cha] CD: phyogs kyi phyogs
ji ltar 'gyur |] N: ji ltar 'gyur ||
E)
gzhan med na] GNP: gzhan med na |
thogs par 'gyur |] GN: thog par 'gyur ||; P: thog par 'gyur |
F)
'gyur te |] G: 'gyur to |H)
rnams las] CD: rnams la (either form seems grammatical)
de'i yin |] GNP: de'i yin
I)
smras pa |] GNP: smras pa
14d
gong bu] N: gang bu
K)
yongs su rtogs pa] GNP: yongs su rtog pa
L)
yin |] CP: yin ||; N: yino ||
M)
dang ||] GN: dang |
sngon po] N: sngon pa

XV

B)
nyes pa] All editions: nges pa
15d
mi sod] N: mi bsod
C)
gom pa gcig bor] GNP: goms pa gcig bor
D)
cha ma zin pa] GNP: cha ma zin pa |
H)
yin na go |] D: yin na go ||
mi 'gyur ro] N: 'gyuro
J)
dag gcig] G: dagcig; P dag cig

XVI

A)
thams cad kyi] N: thams cad kyis
nang na] CD: nang na yang
16b
tshe de yi] GP: che de'i; N: tshe de'i
16c
khyod kyi] GNP: khyod kyis
de mi] CD: de min
D)
bdag gi] GNP: bdag gis
khyod kyi] GNP: khyod kyis
E)
ji ltar 'dod ||] DP: ji ltar 'dod |
F)
zin to ||] DP: zin to |

XVII

B)
de ni de] CD: de ni da ma
D)
yin no ||] GNP: yin no
'di ltar |] CGNP: 'di ltar
17a
rig bzhin ||] GNP: rig bzhin |
17b
bshad zin] GNP: bshad zin nas
E)
bzhin te] D: bzhin ta; GNP: bzhin de
G)
'grub bo ||] D: 'grub bo |
I)
rigs na |] GNP: rig na |
J)
de ltar] GNP: de lta
L)
'di ltar |] GNP: 'di ltar
17d
rtogs ma] GNP: rtog ma
M)
mthong te |] GNP: mthong ste |

XVIII

A)
las sems can] C: las sems can followed by 25 spaces filled with tsegs
'byung gi |] GNP: byung gi
B)
brten pa] GNP: rten pa
de dang] N: de dang followed by 7 spaces filled with tsegs
bshes gnyen la brten pa] N: bshes gnyen la rten pa
sems can rnams kyis] GNP: sems can rnams kyi
ji ltar 'grub] GNP: ji ltar grub
'gyur |] N: 'gyur ||
C)
dbang gis] N: dbang gi
E)
rgyud gzhan gyi] GNP: rgyud gzhan gyis
'byung gi don] GNP: 'byung gi | don
F)
ma log pa na] P: ma log pa ni
kun tu spyod] GNP: kun tu spyad
'dod pa 'dra bar] GNP: 'dod par 'dra bar
mi 'gyur |] N: mi 'gyur
18d
rmi] N: mi
H)
rgyu yin gyi] N: rgyu yin gyis

XIX

A)
ji ltar 'gyur |] GN: ji ltar 'gyur ||
19a
rnam rig gi ||] C: rnam rig gi |; GN: rnam rig gi; P: rnam par rig gi
19b
bya na ||] GP: bya na |
C)
yid kyi dbang gis] GN: yid kyis dbang gi; P: yid kyis dbang gis
gzhan dag gi] GNP: gzhan dag gis
D)
rdzu 'phrul dang] C: rdzu 'phrul dang |
E)
kā tyā'i] GNP: ka ta'i
byin gyi] GNP: byin gyis
brlabs kyis] N: brlab ma gyis
F)
thags zangs ris] GNP: thag bzangs rigs [this is the form found in dictionaries]
G)
'byung ste | des] CD: 'byung ste de
skal ba] All editions: bskal pa
rgyud kyi rgyun chad pa] GNP: rgyud kyis rgyun 'chad pa
zhes bya ba] C: zhas bya ba

XX

20a
khros pas] GNP: khros pa'i
dan ta] GNP: danta
stongs par] NP: stong par
A)
rnam par rig pa'i] GNP: rnam par rig
bye brag gis] G: bye brag gi [folio flip] gi; NP: bye brag gi
mi 'dod na |] GNP: mi 'dod na
B)
kha na ma] GP: kha na
chen po dang] G: chen po dang |
bsgrub pa na |] GNP: sgrub pa na |
bdag nye ba] GNP: bdag nye bar
C)
dan ta] GNP: danta
ling ka'i] NP: lingga'i
dgon pa dang] GNP: dgon pa dang |
tang ka'i] GNP: tangga'i
stongs pa]] GNP: stong pa
D)
zhes smras pa] GNP: zhes rmas pa (this is a rarer verb, but smras agrees with *ukta*; the Buddha's question itself is translated with bka' stsal pa)
F)
rtog ste ||] NP: rtog ste |
drang srong rnams kyis] GNP: drang srong rnams kyi

XXI

A)
sems rig pas] GNP: sems rigs pas
21a
shes pa ni ||] N: shes pa ni |

XXII

A)
rig pa tsam gyis] GNP: rig pa tsam gyi
rnam par nges pa] C: rnam par [folio flip] par nges pa
mi dpogs shing] GNP: mi dpog shing
C)
spyod yul snyam] GNP: spyod yul yin snyam
D)
spyod yul te] GNP: spyod yul yin te

Colophon

dbyig gnyen gyis mdzad pa] GNP: dbyig gnyen gyi mdzad pa'i
len dra] GNP: lendra
ban de] GNP: bande

Sanskrit Reading Text

of the

Viṁśikā-vṛtti

I

... H) nārthaḥ kaścid asti |

II

......

na deśakālaniyamaḥ santānāniyamo na ca |
na ca kr̥tyakriyā yuktā vijñaptir yadi nārthataḥ || 2 ||

......-niyamaḥ santānāniyamaḥ kr̥tyakriyā ca na yujyate ,

III

A) na khalu na yujyate , yasmāt ||

deśādiniyamaḥ siddhas svapnavat

B) svapna iva svapnavat | C) kathaṁ D) tāvat svapne vināpy arthena kvacid eva deśe kiñcid grāmārāmastrīpuruṣādikaṁ dr̥śyate na sarvatra tatraiva ca deśe kadācid dr̥śyate na sarvakālam E) iti siddho vināpy arthena deśakālaniyamaḥ ||

pretavat punaḥ
santānāniyamaḥ ||

F) siddha iti vartate ; G) pretānām iva pretavat | H) kathaṁ siddhaḥ | I) samaṁ

sarvaiḥ pūyanadyādidarśane || 3 ||

J) pūyapūrṇṇā nadī pūyanadī | K) ghr̥taghaṭavat | L) tulyakarmavipākāvasthā hi pretāḥ sarve 'pi samaṁ pūyapūrṇān nadīm paśyanti naika eva | M) yathā pūyapūrṇām evaṁ mūtrapurīṣādipūrṇāṁ daṇḍāsidharaiś ca puruṣair adhiṣṭhitām ity ādigrahaṇena | N) evaṁ santānāniyamo vijñaptīnām asaty apy arthe siddhaḥ ||

IV

svapnopaghātavat kr̥tyakriyā |

A) siddheti veditavyaṁ | B) yathā svapne dvayasamāpattim antareṇa śukravisargalakṣaṇaḥ svapnopaghātaḥ | C) evan tāvad anyānyair dṛṣṭāntair deśakālaniyamādicatuṣṭayaṁ siddhaṁ |

narakavat punaḥ

sarvaṁ

D) siddham iti veditavyaṁ | E) narakeṣv iva narakavat | F) kathaṁ siddhaṁ |

narakapālādidarśane taiś ca bādhane || 4 ||

G) yathā hi narakeṣu nārakāṇāṁ narakapālādidarśanaṁ deśakālaniyamena siddhaṁ | H) śvavāyasāyasaparvatādyāgamanagamanadarśanañ cety ādigrahaṇena | I) sarveṣāñ ca naikasyaiva | J) taiś ca tadbādhanaṁ siddham asatsv api narakapālādiṣu samānasvakarmavipākādhipatyāt | K) tathānyatrāpi sarvam etad deśakālaniyamādicatuṣṭayaṁ siddham iti veditavyaṁ |

L) kim punaḥ kāraṇaṁ narakapālās te ca śvāno vāyasāś ca satvā neṣyante |

M) ayogāt | N) na hi te nārakā yujyante tathaiva tadduḥkhāpratisamvedanāt | O) parasparaṁ yātayatām ime nārakā ime narakapālā iti vyavasthā na syāt | P) tulyākṛtipramāṇabalānāñ ca parasparaṁ yātayatān na tathā bhayaṁ syāt | Q) dāhaduḥkhañ ca pradīptāyām ayomayāṁ bhūmāv asahamānāḥ kathaṁ tatra parān yātayeyuḥ | R) anārakāṇāṁ vā narake kutaḥ sambhavaḥ |

V

A) kathan tāvat tiraścāṁ svarge sambhavaḥ | B) evaṁ narakeṣu tiryakpretaviśeṣāṇāṁ narakapālādīnāṁ sambhavaḥ syāt ||

tiraścāṁ sambhavaḥ svarge yathā na narake tathā |
na pretānāṁ yatas tajjaṁ duḥkhan nānubhavanti te || 5 ||

C) ye hi tiryañcaḥ svarge sambhavanti te tadbhājanalokasukhasaṁvartanīyena karmaṇā tatra sambhūtās tajjaṁ sukhaṁ pratyanubhavanti | D) na caivan narakapālādayo nārakaṁ duḥkhaṁ pratyanubhavanti E) tasmān na tiraścāṁ sambhavo yukto F) nāpi pretānāṁ |

VI

A) teṣān tarhi nārakāṇāṁ karmabhis tatra bhūtaviśeṣāḥ sambhavanti varṇākṛtipramāṇabalaviśiṣṭā ye narakapālādisaṁjñāṁ pratilabhante | B) tathā ca pariṇamanti yad vividhāṁ hastavikṣepādikriyāṁ kurvanto dṛśyante bhayotpādanārthaṁ yathā meṣākṛtayaḥ parvatā āgacchanto gacchantaḥ ayaḥśālmalīvane ca kaṇṭakā adhomukhībhavanta ūrddhamukhībhavantaś ceti | C) na te na sambhavanty eva ||

yadi tatkarmabhis tatra bhūtānāṁ sambhavas tathā |
iṣyate pariṇāmaś ca kiṁ vijñānasya neṣyate || 6 ||

D) vijñānasyaiva tatkarmabhis tathāpariṇāmaḥ kasmān neṣyate | E) kim punar bhūtāni kalpyante || F) api ca ||

VII

karmaṇo vāsanānyatra phalam anyatra kalpyate |
tatraiva neṣyate yatra vāsanā kin nu kāraṇaṁ || 7 ||

A) yena hi karmaṇā nārakāṇāṁ tatra tādṛśo bhūtānāṁ sambhavaḥ kalpyate pariṇāmaś ca tasya karmaṇo vāsanā teṣāṁ vijñānasaṁtānasanniviṣṭā nānyatra , B) yatraiva ca vāsanā tatraiva tasyāḥ phalaṁ tādṛśo vijñānapariṇāmaḥ kin neṣyate | C) yatra vāsanā nāsti tatra tasyāḥ phalaṁ kalpyata iti kim atra kāraṇaṁ |

D) āgamaḥ kāraṇaṁ | E) yadi vijñānam eva rūpādipratibhāsaṁ syān na rūpādiko 'rthas tadā rūpādyāyatanāstitvaṁ bhagavatā noktaṁ syāt |

VIII

A) akāraṇam etat yasmāt ,

rūpādyāyatanāstitvaṁ tadvineyajanam prati |
abhiprāyavaśād uktam upapādukasatvavat || 8 ||

B) yathāsti satva upapāduka ity uktaṁ bhagavatā 'bhiprāyavaśāc cittasantatyanucchedam āyatyām abhipretya |

C) nāstīha satva ātmā vā dharmmās tv ete sahetukāḥ ||

D) iti vacanāt | E) evaṁ rūpādyāyatanāstitvam apy uktaṁ bhagavatā taddeśanāvineyajanam adhikr̥tyety ābhiprāyikaṁ tad vacanaṁ |

IX

A) ko 'trābhiprāyaḥ |

yataḥ svabījād vijñaptir yadābhāsā pravarttate |
dvividhāyatanatvena te tasyā munir abravīt || 9 ||

B) kim uktam bhavati | C) rūpapratibhāsā vijñaptir yataḥ svabījāt pariṇāmaviśeṣaprāptād utpadyate tac ca bījaṁ yatpratibhāsā ca D) sā te tasyā vijñapteś cakṣūrūpāyatanatvena yathākramaṁ bhagavān abravīt | E) evaṁ yāvat spraṣṭavyapratibhāsā vijñaptir yataḥ svabījāt pariṇāmaviśeṣaprāptād utpadyate , tac ca bījaṁ yatpratibhāsā ca F) sā te tasyāḥ kāyaspraṣṭavyāyatanatvena yathākramam bhagavān abravīd G) ity ayam abhiprāyaḥ |

X

A) evaṁ punar abhiprāyavaśena deśayitvā ko guṇaḥ ||

tathā pudgalanairātmyapraveśo hi ||

B) tathā hi deśyamāne pudgalanairātmyaṁ praviśanti | C) dvayaṣaṭkābhyāṁ vijñānaṣaṭkaṁpravartate na tu kaścid eko draṣṭāsti na yāvan mantety evaṁ viditvā ye pudgalanairātmyadeśanāvineyās te pudgalanairātmyaṁ praviśanti ||

anyathā punar
deśanā dharmanairātmyapraveśaḥ ||

D) anyatheti vijñaptimātradeśanā | E) kathaṁ dharmanairātmyapraveśaḥ | F) vijñaptimātram idaṁ rūpādidharmapratibhāsam utpadyate G) na tu rūpādilakṣaṇo dharmaḥ kaścid astīti viditvā |

H) yadi tarhi sarvathā dharmo nāsti tad api vijñaptimātraṁ nāstīti | kathaṁ tarhi vyavasthāpyate |

I) na khalu sarvathā dharmo nāstīty evaṁ dharmanairātmyapraveśo bhavati | J) api tu |

kalpitātmanā , | 10 ||

K) yo bālair dharmāṇāṁ svabhāvo grāhyagrāhakādiḥ parikalpitas tena kalpitenātmanā teṣāṁ nairātmyaṁ L) na tv anabhilāpyenātmanā yo buddhānām viṣaya iti | M) evam vijñaptimātrasyāpi vijñaptyantaraparikalpitenātmanā nairātmyapraveśād vijñaptimātravyavasthāpanayā sarvadharmāṇāṁ nairātmyapraveśo bhavati na tu sarvathā tadastitvāpavādāt | N) itarathā hi vijñapter api vijñaptyantaram arthaḥ syād iti vijñaptimātratvan na sidhyetārthavatītvād vijñaptīnāṁ |

XI

A) kathaṁ punar idaṁ pratyetavyam anenābhiprāyeṇa bhagavatā rūpādyāyatanāstitvam uktaṁ na punaḥ santy eva tāni yāni rūpādivijñaptīnāṁ pratyekaṁ viṣayībhavantīti |

B) yasmān

na tad ekaṁ na cānekaṁ viṣayaḥ paramāṇuśaḥ |
na ca te saṁhatā yasmāt paramāṇur na sidhyati || 11 ||

C) iti | kim uktam bhavati | D) yat tad rūpādikam āyatanaṁ rūpādivijñaptīnāṁ pratyekaṁ viṣayaḥ syāt tad ekaṁ vā syād yathā 'vayavirūpaṁ kalpyate vaiśeṣikaiḥ anekaṁ vā paramāṇuśaḥ saṁhatā vā ta eva paramāṇavaḥ | E) na tāvad ekaṁ viṣayo bhavaty avayavebhyo 'nyasyāvayavirūpasya kvacid apy agrahaṇāt | F) nāpy anekaṁ paramāṇūnāṁ pratyekam agrahaṇāt | G) nāpi te saṁhatā viṣayībhavanti | yasmāt paramāṇur ekaṁ dravyaṁ na sidhyati |

XII

A) kathaṁ na sidhyati |

B) yasmāt |

ṣaṭkena yugapadyogāt paramāṇoḥ ṣaḍaṅśatā ||

C) ṣaḍbhyo digbhyaḥ ṣaḍbhiḥ paramāṇubhir yugapadyoge sati paramāṇoḥ ṣaḍaṅśatā prāpnoti | ekasya yo deśas tatrānyasyāsambhavāt |

ṣaṇṇāṁ samānadeśatvāt piṇḍaḥ syād aṇumātrakaḥ || 12 ||

D) atha ya evaikasya paramāṇor deśaḥ sa eva ṣaṇṇāṁ | E) tena sarveṣāṁ samānadeśatvāt sarvaḥ piṇḍaḥ paramāṇumātraḥ syāt parasparāvyatirekād F) iti na kaścit piṇḍo dr̥śyaḥ syāt | G) naiva hi paramāṇavaḥ saṁyujyante niravayavatvāt | mā bhūd eṣa doṣaprasaṅgaḥ | saṁghātās tu parasparaṁ saṁyujyanta iti kāśmīravaibhāṣikās | H) te idaṁ praṣṭavyāḥ | I) yaḥ paramāṇūnāṁ saṁghāto na sa tebhyo 'rthāntaram iti ||

XIII

paramāṇor asaṁyoge tatsaṁghāte 'sti kasya saḥ ||

A) saṁyoga iti varttate |

na cānavayavatvena tatsaṁyogo na sidhyati || 13 ||

B) atha saṁghātā apy anyonyaṁ na saṁyujyante na tarhi paramāṇūnāṁ niravayavatvāt saṁyogo na sidhyatīti vaktavyaṁ | sāvayavasyāpi hi saṁghātasya saṁyogānabhyupagamāt | C) ataḥ paramāṇur ekaṁ dravyaṁ na sidhyati | D) yadi ca paramāṇoḥ saṁyoga iṣyate yadi vā neṣyate |

XIV

digbhāgabhedo yasyāsti tasyaikatvan na yujyate |

A) anyo hi paramāṇoḥ pūrvadigbhāgo yāvad adhodigbhāga iti digbhāgabhede sati kathaṁ tadātmakasya paramāṇor ekatvaṁ yokṣyate |

chāyāvr̥tī kathaṁ vā |

B) yady ekaikasya paramāṇor digbhāgabhedo na syād ādityodaye katham anyatra pārśve chāyā bhavaty anyatrātapaḥ | C) na hi tasyānyaḥ pradeśo 'sti yatrātapo na syāt | D) āvaraṇañ ca kathaṁ bhavati paramāṇoḥ paramāṇvantareṇa yadi digbhāgabhedo neṣyate | E) na hi kaścid anyaḥ parabhāgo 'sti yatrāgamanād anyenānyasya pratighātaḥ syāt | F) asati ca pratighāte sarveṣāṁ samānadeśatvāt sarvaḥ saṁghātaḥ paramāṇumātraḥ syād ity uktaṁ |

G) kim evaṁ neṣyate piṇḍasya te chāyāvṛtī na paramāṇor iti |

H) kiṁ khalu paramāṇubhyo 'nyaḥ piṇḍa iṣyate yasya te syātāṁ |

I) nety āha |

anyo na piṇḍaś cen na tasya te || 14 ||

J) yadi nānyaḥ paramāṇubhyaḥ piṇḍa iṣyate na te tasyeti siddham bhavati |

K) sanniveśaparikalpa eṣaḥ | paramāṇuḥ saṁghāta iti vā kim anayā cintayā | lakṣaṇan tu rūpādīnāṁ na pratiṣidhyate |

L) kim punas teṣāṁ lakṣaṇaṁ

M) cakṣurādiviṣayatvaṁ nīlāditvañ ca

N) tad evedaṁ sampradhāryate | yat tac cakṣurādīnāṁ viṣayo nīlapītādikam iṣyate kin tad ekaṁ dravyam atha vā tad anekam iti |

XV

A) kiñ cātaḥ |

B) anekatve doṣa uktaḥ ||

ekatve na krameṇetir yugapan na grahāgrahau |
vicchinnānekavṛttiś ca sūkṣmānīkṣā ca no bhavet || 15 ||

C) yadi yāvad avicchinnaṁ nīlādikañ cakṣuṣo viṣayas tad ekaṁ dravyaṁ kalpyate pṛthivyāṁ krameṇetir na syāt | gamanam ity arthaḥ | sakṛtpādakṣepeṇa sarvasya gatatvāt | D) arvāgbhāgasya ca grahaṇaṁ parabhāgasya cāgrahaṇaṁ yugapan na syāt | na hi tasyaiva tadānīṁ grahaṇañ cāgrahaṇañ ca yuktam |

E) vicchinnasya cānekasya hastyaśvādikasyaikatra vṛttir na syāt | F) yatraiva hy ekan tatraivāparam iti kathan tayor vicchedo yujyate | G) katham vā tad ekaṁ yat prāptañ ca tābhyāṁ na ca prāptam antarāle tacchūnyagrahaṇāt | H) sūkṣmāṇāñ codakajantūnāṁ sthūlaiḥ samānarūpāṇām anīkṣaṇaṁ na syāt | yadi lakṣaṇabhedād eva dravyāntaratvaṁ kalpyate , nānyathā , I) tasmād avaśyaṁ paramāṇuśo bhedaḥ kalpayitavyaḥ | J) sa caiko na sidhyati | K) tasyāsiddhau rūpādīnāṁ cakṣurādiviṣayatvam asiddham L) iti siddhaṁ vijñaptimātram bhavatīti |

XVI

A) pramāṇavaśād astitvaṁ nāstitvaṁ vā nirddhāryate | sarveṣāñ ca pramāṇānāṁ pratyakṣam pramāṇaṁ gariṣṭham B) ity asaty arthe katham iyaṁ buddhir bhavatīdaṁ me pratyakṣam iti ||

pratyakṣabuddhiḥ svapnādau yathā |

C) vināpy artheneti pūrvam eva jñāpitaṁ |

sā ca yadā tadā |
na so 'rtho dṛśyate tasya pratyakṣatvaṁ kathaṁ mataṁ
|| 16 ||

D) yadā ca sā pratyakṣabuddhir bhavatīdaṁ me pratyakṣam iti tadā na so 'rtho dṛśyate manovijñānenaiva paricchedāc cakṣurvijñānasya ca tadā niruddhatvād E) iti kathaṁ tasya pratyakṣatvam iṣṭaṁ | F) viśeṣeṇa tu kṣaṇikavādino yasya tadānīṁ niruddham eva tad rūpaṁ rasādikaṁ vā |

XVII

A) nānanubhūtam manovijñānena smaryate | B) ity avaśyam arthānubhavena bhavitavyaṁ tac ca darśanam ity C) evaṁ tadviṣayasya rūpādeḥ pratyakṣatvaṁ mataṁ |

D) asiddham idam anubhūtasyārthasya smaraṇam bhavatīti | yasmāt |

uktaṁ yathā tadābhāsā vijñaptiḥ ||

E) vināpy arthena yathārthābhāsā cakṣurvijñānādikā vijñaptir utpadyate tathoktaṁ ||

smaraṇaṁ tataḥ |

F) tato hi vijñapteḥ smr̥tisamprayuktā tatpratibhāsaiva rūpādivikalpikā manovijñaptir utpadyata G) iti na smr̥tyutpādād arthānubhavaḥ sidhyati |

H) yadi yathā svapne vijñaptir abhūtārthaviṣayā tathā jāgrato 'pi syāt I) tathaiva tadabhāvaṁ lokaḥ svayam avagacchet | J) na caivam bhavati | K) tasmān na svapna ivārthopalabdhiḥ sarvā nirarthikā |

L) idam ajñāpakaṁ | yasmāt |

svapnadr̥gviṣayābhāvaṁ nāprabuddho 'vagacchati || 17 ||

M) evaṁ vitathavikalpābhyāsavāsanānidrayā prasupto lokaḥ svapna ivābhūtam artham paśyann N) aprabuddhas tadabhāvaṁ yathāvan nāvagacchati , O) yadā tu tatpratipakṣalokottaranirvikalpajñānalābhāt prabuddho bhavati tadā tatpr̥ṣṭhalabdhaśuddhalaukikajñānasammukhībhāvād viṣayābhāvaṁ yathāvad avagacchatīti samānam etat |

XVIII

A) yadi svasantānapariṇāmaviśeṣād eva satvānām arthapratibhāsā vijñaptaya utpadyante nārthaviśeṣāt | B) tadā ya eṣa pāpakalyāṇamitrasaṁparkāt sadasaddharmaśravaṇāc ca vijñaptiniyamaḥ satvānāṁ sa kathaṁ sidhyati , asati sadasatsaṁparke taddeśanāyāñ ca |

anyonyādhipatitvena vijñaptiniyamo mithaḥ ||

C) sarveṣāṁ hi satvānām anyonyavijñaptyādhipatyena mitho vijñapter niyamo bhavati yathāyogaṁ | D) mitha iti parasparataḥ | E) ataḥ santānāntaravijñaptiviśeṣāt santānāntare vijñaptiviśeṣa utpadyate nārthaviśeṣāt |

F) yadi yathā svapne nirarthikā vijñaptir evañ jāgrato 'pi syāt kasmāt kuśalākuśalasamudācāre suptāsuptayos tulyaṁ phalam iṣṭāniṣṭam āyatyān na bhavati |

G) yasmāt |

middhenopahatañ cittaṁ svapne tenāsamaṁ phalaṁ || 18 ||

H) idam atra kāraṇaṁ na tv arthasadbhāvaḥ |

XIX

A) yadi vijñaptimātram evedaṁ na kasyacit kāyo 'sti na vāk katham upakramyamāṇānām aurabhrikādibhir urabhrādīnāṁ maraṇam bhavati , B) atatkr̥te vā tanmaraṇe katham aurabhrikādīnāṁ prāṇātipātāvadyena yogo bhavati ||

maraṇaṁ paravijñaptiviśeṣād vikriyā yathā |
smr̥tilopādikānyeṣāṁ piśācādimanovaśāt || 19 ||

C) yathā hi piśācādimanovaśād anyeṣāṁ smr̥tilopasvapnadarśanabhūtagrahāveśavikārā bhavanti | D) r̥ddhivanmanovaśāc ca | E) yathā sāraṇasyāryamahākātyāyanādhiṣṭhānāt svapnadarśanaṁ | F) āraṇyakarṣimanaḥpradoṣāc ca vemacitriṇaḥ parājayaḥ | G) tathā paravijñaptiviśeṣādhipatyāt pareṣāṁ jīvitendriyavirodhinī kācid vikriyotpadyate yayā sabhāgasantativicchedākhyam maraṇam bhavatīti veditavyaṁ |

XX

kathaṁ vā daṇḍakāraṇyaśūnyatvam r̥ṣikopataḥ |

A) yadi paravijñaptiviśeṣādhipatyāt satvānāṁ maraṇaṁ neṣyate | B) manodaṇḍasya hi mahāsāvadyatvaṁ sādhayatā bhagavatopālir gr̥hapatiḥ pr̥ṣṭaḥ C) kaccit te gr̥hapate śrutaṁ kena tāni daṇḍakāraṇyāni mātaṅgāraṇyāni kaliṅgāraṇyāni śūnyāni medhyībhūtāni | D) tenoktaṁ śrutaṁ me bho gautama r̥ṣīṇāṁ manaḥpradoṣeṇeti ||

manodaṇḍo mahāvadyaḥ kathaṁ vā tena sidhyati || 20 ||

E) yady evaṁ kalpyate , tadabhiprasannair amānuṣais tadvāsinaḥ satvā utsāditā na tv r̥ṣīṇāṁ manaḥpradoṣān mr̥tā ity F) evaṁ sati kathaṁ tena karmaṇā manodaṇḍaḥ kāyavāgdaṇḍābhyām mahāvadyatamaḥ siddho bhavati | G) tan manaḥpradoṣamātreṇa tāvatāṁ satvānāṁ maraṇāt sidhyati |

XXI

A) yadi vijñaptimātram evedaṁ paracittavidaḥ kiṁ paracittaṁ jānanty , atha na , B) kiñ cātaḥ I C) yadi na jānanti kathaṁ paracittavido bhavanti | D) atha jānanti |

paracittavidāṁ jñānam ayathārthaṁ kathaṁ yathā ,
svacittajñānaṁ

E) tad api katham ayathārthaṁ |

ajñānād yathā buddhasya gocaraḥ || 21 ||

F) yathā tan nirabhilāpyenātmanā buddhānāṁ gocaraḥ | tathā tadajñānāt | tad ubhayaṁ na yathārthaṁ G) vitathapratibhāsatayā H) grāhyagrāhakavikalpasyāprahīṇatvāt |

XXII

A) anantaviniścayaprabhedāgādhagāmbhīryāyāṁ vijñaptimātratāyāṁ |

vijñaptimātratāsiddhiḥ svaśaktisadr̥śī mayā |
kr̥teyaṁ sarvathā sā tu na cintyā ,

B) sarvaprakārā tu sā mādr̥śaiś cintayituṁ na śakyā tarkkāviṣayatvāt | C) kasya punaḥ sā sarvathā gocara ity āha |

buddhagocaraḥ , | 22 ||

D) buddhānāṁ hi sā bhagavatāṁ sarvaprakāraṁ gocaraḥ sarvākārasarvajñeyajñānāvighātād iti ||

viṁśikā vijñaptimātratāsiddhiḥ
kr̥tir iyam ācāryavasubandhoḥ ||

English Reading Text

of the

Viṁśikā-vṛtti

I

[Vasubandhu]

A) The Great Vehicle teaches that what belongs to the triple world is established as Manifestation-Only, because it is stated in scripture: B) "O Sons of the Conqueror, what belongs to the triple world is mind-only." C) Mind, thought, cognition and manifestation are synonyms. D) And here this 'mind' intends the inclusion of the concomitants [of mind]. E) "Only" is stated in order to rule out external objects. F) This cognition itself arises having the appearance of an external object. G) For example, it is like those with an eye disease seeing non-existent hair, a [double] moon and so on, but H) there is no [real] object at all.

II

[Objection:]

A) To this it is objected:

If manifestation does not [arise] from an external object,
it is not reasonable that there be restriction as to time
and place, nor nonrestriction as to personal continuum,
nor causal efficacy. [2]

B) What is being stated here? C) If there is the arisal of manifestation of material form and so on without any external object of material form and so on, and [consequently the manifestation] does not [arise] from a [real] external object of material form and so on, D) why does [such a manifestation] arise in a particular place, and not everywhere; E) why does it arise only in that place at some time, not always; and F) why does it arise without restriction in the minds of all those present there in that place at that time, and not in [the minds] of just a few? G) For instance, while a hair and so on may appear in the mind of one with eye disease, it does not [appear] to others [free of that disease].

H) Why is it that the hair, bee and so on which appear to one with eye disease have no causal efficacy of a hair and so on, while for those others without [eye disease, those hairs, bees and so forth which appear to them] do have [causal efficacy]? I) The food, drink, clothing, poison, weapons and so on seen in a dream do not have causal efficacy [to address] hunger, thirst and the like, but those others not [in a dream] do have such [causal efficacy]. J) A mirage city, being non-existent, does not have the causal efficacy of a city, but other [cities] not [unreal like] that do. K) If these [things like dream food] resemble the non-existent in lacking any [real external] object, restriction as to time and place, nonrestriction as to personal continuum, and causal efficacy are not reasonable.

III

[Vasubandhu]

A) They are certainly not unreasonable, since:

Restriction as to place and so on is proved, as with dreams.

[3ab]

B) "As with dreams" means as in a dream. CD) Well, how, first of all, [do you explain that] even without an external object, some village, grove, man, woman or the like is seen in a dream at a particular place, rather than everywhere, and at that particular place at some specific time, rather than always? E) For this reason, restriction as to time and place is established, even in the absence of an external object.

Moreover, nonrestriction to personal continuum [is proved] as with hungry ghosts. [3bc]

F) "Is proved" is carried over [from the previous foot]. G) "As with hungry ghosts" means as in the case of hungry ghosts. H) How is this proved? I) Collectively

In their all seeing the river of pus and so on. [3cd]

J) "The river of pus" means a river filled with pus, K) as [one says] a pot of ghee [when one means a pot filled with ghee]. L) For hungry ghosts in a state of equally experiencing fruition of their actions collectively *all* see the river filled with pus, not just one of them alone. M) The word "and so on" is mentioned to indicate that as [they see the river] filled with pus, they [also see it] filled with urine, feces and the like, and guarded by persons holding staffs and swords. N) Thus the non-restriction of manifestations to [a specific] personal continuum is proved even without the existence of an external object.

IV

Causal efficacy [is proved] as in ejaculation in a dream. [4ab]

A) "Is proved" is to be understood. B) [Causal efficacy is established] as with ejaculation in a dream [that is, a wet dream], which is characterized by the emission of semen in a dream in the absence of [actual] sexual union. C) In this way at the outset is proved, through these various examples, the four-fold [characterization, namely] the restriction to time and place and the rest.

And again as with hell all [four aspects are proved]. [4bc]

D) "Are proved" is to be understood. E) "As with hell" means like in the hells. F) How are they proved?

In the seeing of the hell guardians and so on, and in being tortured by them. [4cd]

G) Just as it is proved that in the hells hell beings see the hell guardians and so on with restriction as to time and place H) —"and so on" means that they see the dogs, crows, the iron mountains and so on coming and going— I) and all [hell beings see these], not merely one, J) and [just as it is] proved that they are tortured by them, even though the hell guardians and so on do not exist, because of the domination of the generalized common fruition of their individual karmic deeds— K) Just so it should be understood that the entirety of this four-fold [characterization, namely] the restriction to time and place and the rest, is proved elsewhere too [and not only in the separate examples].

[Objection]

L) For what reason, then, do you not accept the hell guardians, and dogs and crows, as really existent beings?

[Vasubandhu]

M) Because it is not reasonable. N) For it is not reasonable for those [guardians and so on] to be hell beings, since they do not experience the sufferings of that [place] in precisely that same way. O) If they were torturing each other, there would be no differentiation that 'these are the hell beings; these the hell guardians.' P) And if those of equal form, size and strength were torturing each other, they would not be so very afraid. Q) And how could [those guardians], unable to tolerate the suffering of burning on a flaming iron ground, torture others there? R) On the other hand, how could non-hell beings be born in hell [in the first place]?

V

[Objection]

A) [Well,] to begin, how [—as you admit as well—] could animals be born in heaven? B) In the same way, animals and certain hungry ghosts might be born in the hells as hell guardians and others.

[Vasubandhu]

Animals are not born in hell as they are in heaven,
Nor are hungry ghosts, since they do not experience the suffering produced there. [5]

C) For, those who are born in heaven as animals, being born there through their karmic deeds conducive to happiness [performed] in the Receptacle World, experience the happiness produced there [in heaven], D) but the hell guardians and so on do not experience hellish suffering in a similar fashion. E) Therefore, it is not reasonable that animals are born [in hell], F) nor is it so for hungry ghosts.

VI

[Objection]

A) Then, particular types of gross material elements arise there through the karmic deeds of those hell beings, which, particularized as to color, form, size and strength, obtain the designations 'hell guardian' and so on. B) And they transform in such a manner that they appear performing activities like waving their hands and so on, in order to instill fear, as mountains in the shape of rams coming and going and thorns in the forest of iron thorn trees turning themselves down and turning themselves up [likewise appear in hell instilling fear]. C) Therefore, it is not that those [hell guardians and so on] are not born at all.

[Vasubandhu]

If you accept that gross material elements arise there in this fashion through the karmic deeds of those [beings],
And [you accept their] transformation, why do you not accept [the transformation] of cognition? [6]

D) Why do you not accept that the transformation thus brought about by the karmic deeds of those [beings] is [a transformation] of cognition itself? E) Why, moreover, are gross material elements imagined [to play any role at all]? F) What is more:

VII

The perfuming of the karmic deed you imagine to be elsewhere than the result;
What is the reason you do not accept [that the result is] in precisely the same location where the perfuming [takes place]? [7]

A) You imagine such an arising and transformation of gross material elements of hell beings there [in hell] as due to their karmic deeds, while the perfuming of those karmic deeds is lodged in their individual continua of cognition, not elsewhere. B) So why do you not accept that such a transformation of cognition as the result of those [karmic deeds] is precisely where the perfuming itself is? C) For what reason, in this case, do you imagine that the result of those [karmic deeds] is somewhere where the perfuming is not?

[Objection]

D) The reason is scripture. E) If there were nothing but cognition with the appearance of material form and the rest, and no external objects characterized as material form and the rest, then the Blessed One would not have spoken of the existence of the sense-fields of material form and the rest.

VIII

[Vasubandhu]

A) This is not a reason, since:

The existence of the sense-fields of material form and the rest were spoken of [by the Blessed One] with a special intention directed toward the individual to be guided by that [teaching], as [in the case of the mention of] beings born by spontaneous generation. [8]

B) By way of example, the Blessed One with a special intention said "There are beings of spontaneous birth," intending [allusion to] the nonannihilation of the continuum of mind in the future. D) [We know this] because of the [scriptural] statement:

C) Here [in our teaching] there is no being or self,
but [only] these elemental factors of existence along with their causes.

E) Thus, although the Blessed One did speak of the existence of the sense-fields of form and the rest, that [scriptural] statement is of special intention since it is directed toward the individual who is to be guided by that teaching.

IX

A) In this regard, what is the special intention?

A manifestation arises from its own proper seed, having an appearance corresponding to that [external object]. The Sage spoke of the two [seed and appearance] as the dual sense field of that [manifestation]. [9]

B) What is being stated? C) The proper seed from which—when it has attained a particular transformation—arises a manifestation having the appearance of visible form, and that as which this [cognition] appears: D) the Blessed One spoke of these two as, respectively, the sense field of visual perception ["seeing eye" = seed] and the sense field of visible form [= the object] related to that manifestation. E) The same [applies to all items in the stock list] up to: The Blessed One spoke of the proper seed from which—when it has attained a particular transformation—arises a manifestation having the appearance of the tangible, and that as which this [manifestation] appears: F) [the Blessed One spoke] of these two as, respectively, the sense field of tangible perception ["body" = seed] and the sense field of the tangible [= the object] related to that [manifestation]. G) This is the special intention.

X

[Objection]

A) And what is the advantage of having explained things in this way by recourse to special intention?

[Vasubandhu]

> **For in this way there is understanding of the selflessness of persons.** [10ab]

B) For when it is being taught in this way [those individuals to be guided] understand the idea of the selflessness of persons. C) The six cognitions come about from the two sets of six [= the twelve sense-fields], but when they understand that there is no distinct seer at all—[and all members of the stock list] up to—no distinct thinker, those who are to be guided by the teaching of the selflessness of persons understand the idea of the selflessness of persons.

> **Moreover, teaching in another way leads to the understanding of the selflessness of elemental factors of existence.** [10bcd]

D) "In another way" refers to the teaching of Manifestation-Only. E) How does this lead to understanding the selflessness of elemental factors of existence? F) [One understands this by] knowing that this Manifestation-Only arises with the semblance of elemental factors of existence such as material form and the rest, G) but actually there is no existing elemental factor of existence having as its characteristic mark material form and the rest.

[Objection]

H) If, then, no elemental factor of existence exists in any fashion, Manifestation-Only does not exist either. How, then, could [your position] be established?

[Vasubandhu]

I) It is not the case that one comes to understand the selflessness of elemental factors of existence by thinking that the elemental factors of existence do not exist in any fashion at all. J) But rather [such understanding comes in thinking that elemental factors of existence exist only]:

In terms of an imagined self. [10d]

K) The reference is to the selflessness of those elemental factors of existence the intrinsic nature of which—characterized by subject and object and so on—fools fantasize in terms of an imagined self. L) [The reference] is not to [the selflessness of elemental factors of existence] in terms of the inexpressible self, which is the domain of the Buddhas. M) In this way, Manifestation-Only also leads to an understanding of the selflessness of all elemental factors of existence through the establishment of the fact of Manifestation-Only because of an understanding of selflessness in terms of a self fantasized by another manifestation, not because of a denial of the existence of those [elemental factors of existence] in each and every respect. N) For otherwise one manifestation would have another manifestation as its external object, and therefore the fact of Manifestation-Only could not be proved, because manifestations would possess external objects.

XI

[Objection]

A) How, then, should one understand this, namely, that while the Blessed One spoke of the existence of the sense-fields of visible form and the rest with this special intention, those things which come to be the corresponding sense objects of the manifestations of visible form and the rest do not actually exist at all?

[Vasubandhu]

B) Since:

> **That [sense-field of form and the rest] is not a unitary nor atomically plural sense object, neither are those [atoms] compounded, since the atom [itself] is not proved.** [11]

C) What is stated here? D) Whatever sense-field, consisting of visible form and the rest, would be the corresponding sense object of the manifestations of visible form and the rest, would be either unitary—as the Vaiśeṣikas imagine material form as a part-possessing whole—or it would be atomically plural, or it would be compounded of those very atoms themselves. E) First of all, the sense object is not unitary, because there is no apprehension anywhere at all of a material form as a part-possessing whole separate from its parts. F) Nor is it plural, because there is no apprehension of atoms individually. G) Nor would those [atoms], compounded, come to be the sense object, since the atom is not proved to be a singular substance.

XII

[Objection]

A) How is [the atom as a singular substance] not proved?

[Vasubandhu]

B) Since:

Because [either] in the simultaneous conjunction with a group of six [other atoms], the atom [would have to] have six parts, [12ab]

C) If there were simultaneous conjunction with six atoms from the six directions [of possible orientation], this would result in the atom having six parts, because where there is one thing another cannot arise.

[Or] because, the six being in a common location, the cluster would be the extent of a [single] atom. [12cd]

D) Or, the place in which there are six atoms would be precisely the same as the place of the single atom. E) For this [reason], because all of them would be in a common location, the entire cluster would be the extent of a [single] atom, because they would not exclude one another. F) Thus no cluster would be visible at all. G) The Kashmiri Vaibhāṣikas say: "Atoms do not at all conjoin, because of being partless—absolutely not! But compounded things do conjoin one with another." H) They should be questioned as follows: I) Since a compound of atoms is not something separate from those [atoms],

XIII

Given that there is no conjunction of atoms, what is [conjoining] when those [atoms] are compounded? [13ab]

A) "Conjoining" is carried over [from the previous].

But it is also not due to their partlessness that the conjunction of those [atoms] is not proved. [13cd]

B) If you now were to claim that even compounds do not conjoin with one another, then you [Kashmiri Vaibhāṣikas] should not say that the conjunction of atoms is not proved because of their partlessness, for a conjunction of the compounded, even with parts, is not admitted. C) Therefore, the atom is not proved as a singular substance. D) And whether a conjunction of atoms is accepted or not:

XIV

It is not reasonable that something with spatial differentiation be singular. [14ab]

A) If there were spatial differentiation of an atom—namely, the front part is different [and so are all the other sides] including the bottom part—how would the singularity of an atom with that [multiple] nature be reasonable?

Or how is there shadow and obstruction? [14c]

B) If no single atom were to have spatial differentiation, how is it that when the sun rises in one place, there is shadow in one place, sunshine in another? C) For that [atom] does not have another portion on which there would be no sunshine. D) And how is an atom obstructed by another atom if spatial differentiation is not accepted? E) For [an atom] has no other separate part whatsoever, from contact with which one [atom] would be resisted by another. F) And if there were no resistance, then because all of them would share a common location, the entire compound would be the extent of a [single] atom, as has [already] been discussed [in verse 12cd, above].

[Objection]

G) Do you not accept in this way that the two, shadow and obstruction, belong to the cluster, not to the atom?

[Vasubandhu]

H) Do you, for your part, accept that the cluster which would possess those two [shadow and obstruction] is something other than the atoms ?

[Opponent]

I) We say: no.

[Vasubandhu]

If the cluster is not other [than the atoms], the two [shadow and obstruction] would not be [properties] of that [cluster]. [14cd]

J) If you do not accept the cluster as something other than the atoms, then it is proved that the two [shadow and obstruction] are not [properties] of that [cluster].

[Objection]

K) This is mere imaginative speculation about construction. Why do you have this worry about whether it is an atom or a compound? In any case, the characteristic of visible form and the rest is not negated.

[Vasubandhu]

L) Then what *is* their characteristic?

[Objection]

M) Being a sense-field of visual perception and the rest, and blueness and the like [are the characteristic of visible form].

[Vasubandhu]

N) This is precisely what is being determined: is the sense-field of visual perception and the rest you accept as blue, yellow and so on a single substance, or rather multiple?

XV

[Objection]

A) And what [follows] from this?

[Vasubandhu]

B) The fault if it is [judged to be] multiple has already been discussed.

If [the sense object] were singular, there would be no gradual motion, no simultaneous apprehension and non-apprehension, nor divided multiple existence, nor the invisible microscopic. [15]

C) If one imagines the visual sense-object, blue and the rest, as long as it is undivided, to be a single substance, there would not be gradual motion on the ground—going, that is to say—because everything would be traversed with a single foot-step. D) And the apprehension of a facing portion and the non-apprehension of the non-facing portion would not be simultaneous, because the apprehension and non-apprehension of the very same thing at that [same] time is not reasonable.

E) And there would be no existence of divided and multiple elephants, horses and so on in a single place; F) because one thing would be just precisely where another is, how could a division between them be reasonable? G) Or on the other hand, how is [it reasonable that] that [place] is single which is [both] occupied by those two [elephant and horse] and not occupied, since one apprehends that the gap between them is empty of the two? H) And, if you were to imagine [the two] to have a difference in substance purely because of a distinction in characteristic feature, not otherwise, microscopic aquatic creatures, having forms like macroscopic [creatures], would not be invisible.

I) Therefore [since this is not the case], one must certainly imagine a distinction atomically. J) And that [atom] is not proved to be singular. K) Since [the singular atom] is not proven, the fact that visible form—and the rest—are sense-fields of the visual—and the rest—is unproven; L) therefore Manifestation-Only comes to be proved.

XVI

[Objection]

A) Existence or non-existence is settled on the strength of the valid means of cognition, and of all valid means of cognition, direct perception is the most important valid means of cognition. B) Therefore, if an external object does not exist, how does this awareness come about, namely 'this is before my eyes'?

[Vasubandhu]

> **The idea that there is direct perception [of the external object takes place] as in a dream and so on.** [16ab]

C) I already earlier made the point that "Even without an external object" [is understood].

Additionally, that external object is not seen [at the moment] when one has [the idea that there is direct perception of an external object]; [so] how can you consider that [the external object] is directly perceived? [16bcd]

D) And [at the moment] when that idea [that there is] direct perception [of the external object] comes about with the thought "This is my direct perception," that external object is not seen [at that same moment], because the discerning takes place only by means of mental cognition, and because at that time the visual cognition [which precedes the mental cognition] has ceased. E) Given this, how can you accept that that [object] is directly perceived? F) What is more, [this holds] especially for one who advocates the momentariness [of all things], for whom [the respective] visible form, or flavor and the rest, has [already] entirely ceased at that time.

XVII

[Objection]

A) What was not [previously] experienced cannot be recollected by mental cognition. B) Therefore, there must be experience of an external object, and that is spoken of as 'seeing'. C) In this way I consider it to be a case of an direct perception of that sense-object, [namely] material form and the rest.

[Vasubandhu]

D) This [argument about] recollection [being] of an experienced external object is unproved, since:

As I discussed, manifestation has the appearance of that [external object]. [17ab]

E) I have discussed how, even in the absence of an external object, a manifestation consisting of visual cognition and so forth arises with the appearance of an external object.

Recollection [comes] from that. [17b]

F) For from that manifestation arises a mental manifestation associated with memory, which has precisely the appearance of that [material form] and conceptually fantasizes itself [to refer to] material form and so on; G) thus the arisal of a memory does not prove the experience of an external object.

[Objection]

H) If a manifestation were to have as its sense-object an unreal external object also for one awake, just as is the case in a dream, I) in precisely that way everyone would understand by themselves the non-existence of that [external object]. J) But that is not how it is. K) Therefore, it is not so that all referential objectifications of external objects are, as is the case in a dream, [actually] devoid of external objects.

[Vasubandhu]

L) You cannot draw a conclusion from this, since:

One who is not awake does not understand the non-existence of a sense-object seen in a dream. [17cd]

M) Just so everyone, asleep with the sleep of repeated perfuming of erroneous conceptual fantasy, sees unreal external objects, as in a dream; N) being unawakened, they do not properly understand the non-existence of the [external object]. O) But when they are awakened through the acquisition of supramundane non-discriminative insight which is the antidote to that [erroneous imagination], then they properly understand the non-existence of the sense-object because the subsequently obtained pure worldly insight becomes present. This [situation] is the same.

XVIII

[Objection]

A) If manifestations with the appearance of external objects were to arise for beings only through particular transformations of their own mental continua, not through particular external objects, B) then how is it proved that association with bad or good spiritual guides, and hearing true and false teachings, shape the manifestations of beings, if that association with the good and the bad and that teaching do not [actually] exist?

> **Mutual shaping of manifestation is due to their influence on each other.** [18ab]

C) Because all beings exert an influence on each others' manifestations, there comes to be mutual shaping of manifestation, according to the circumstances. D) "Mutually" means "reciprocally." E) Therefore, a distinct manifestation arises within one mental continuum because of a distinct manifestation within another mental continuum, not because of a distinct external object.

[Objection]

F) If [as you claim] a manifestation were devoid of an external object likewise also for one awake, as is the case in a dream, why do those asleep and those not asleep not come in the future to have the same [karmic] result, desired and undesired [respectively], of [their] wholesome and unwholesome behavior?

[Vasubandhu]

G) Since:

When one dreams, the mind is overpowered by sloth; thus the result is not the same. [18cd]

H) This is the cause in this case, and not [some alleged] real existence of an external object.

XIX

[Objection]

A) If this [world] is nothing but Manifestation-Only, and no one has a body or voice, how does the death of rams and others being attacked by butchers come about? B) Or if their death is not due to those [butchers], how does there come to be a connection between the butchers and the crime of taking life?

Death is a transformation due to a particular manifestation of another, just as the transformation of memory loss and the like of others is due to the mental force of demons and so on. [19]

C) Just as, due to the mental force of demons and so on others come to experience dislocations [including] memory loss, dream visions and possession by ghouls of illness, D) and [this also takes place] due to the mental force of those possessed of superpowers— E) For example, Sāraṇa had a dream vision due to the controlling power of Ārya-Mahākātyāyana, F) and the conquest of Vemacitrin was due to the hostility of the forest ascetics— G) Just so, it is due to the influence of a particular manifestation of another that there arises some transformation of others obstructing the life force, by which there comes to be death, designated as the cutting off of related [mental] continuities. This is how it should be understood.

Otherwise, how did the Daṇḍaka forest become emptied by the sages' anger? [20ab]

A) If you do not accept that beings die because of the influence of a particular manifestation of another [how do you account for what happened in the Daṇḍaka forests?]. B) For the Blessed One, in proving that mental violence is highly objectionable, asked the householder Upāli: C) "Have you heard anything, householder? By whom were the Daṇḍaka forests, the Mātaṅga forests, and the Kaliṅga forests emptied and made ritually pure?" E) He said: "I have heard, O Gautama, it was through the mental hostility of the sages."

XX

Or how does that prove mental violence is a great violation? [20cd]

E) If you were to imagine as follows: beings dwelling there were annihilated by non-humans favorable to those [sages], rather than dying due to the mental hostility of the sages— F) if such were the case, how does that action prove mental violence to be a much greater violation than physical or verbal violence? G) That is proved by the death of so many beings solely on account of mental hostility.

XXI

[Objection]

A) If this [world] is nothing but Manifestation-Only, do then "those who know other minds" [really] know other minds, or not? B) And what [follows] from this? C) If they do not know, how do they become those who [are spoken of as ones who] know others minds? D) Or they do know [which is only possible if external objects do really exist, in which case]:

How is the knowledge of those who know other minds inconsistent with reality?
[Reply:] **It is as with knowledge of one's own mind.** [21abc]

E) How is that [knowledge of one's own mind] also inconsistent with reality?

Because one does not know [other minds or even one's own] in the way that [such knowing of minds] is the scope of a Buddha. [21cd]

F) Because we do not know that in the way that that [knowledge] is the scope of the buddhas, with respect to its nature as inexpressible. Both [knowledges, of one's own mind and of those of others,] are inconsistent with reality, G) because [all that non-buddhas are able to know is an] erroneous appearance. H) This is because they fail to reject the conceptual fantasy of subject and object.

XXII

A) Because [the idea of] Manifestation-Only has unfathomable depth, its explanations and divisions endless,

I have composed this proof of [the World as] Manifestation-Only according to my ability, but that [fact that the World is nothing but Manifestation-Only] is not conceivable in its entirety. [22abcd]

B) However, that [idea of Manifestation-Only] cannot be conceived in all its aspects by those like me, because it is beyond the domain of logical reasoning. C) For whom, then, is this [idea] in all respects the [proper] scope? We reply:

It is the scope of the buddhas. [22d]

D) For it is the scope of the buddhas, the Blessed Ones, in all aspects, because their knowledge of all objects of knowledge in all ways is unobstructed.

Colophon:

This is the Proof of [the World as] Manifestation-Only in Twenty Verses
A composition of the Master Vasubandhu.